Conversations
with the
Tarot

A Dialogue with each of the 22 Major Arcana

Pitisci

Conversations with the Tarot Copyright © 2023, by Vincent Pitisci

Illustrations from the Rider Waite Tarot Deck® reproduced by permission of U.S. Games Systems, Inc., Stamford, CT 06902 USA. Copyright ©1970 by U.S. Games Systems, Inc.

All rights reserved. No part of this book may be reproduced in any form, except brief excerpts for purpose of review without written permission from the author.

Dedication

To the 22 Major Arcana for their help in putting this book together.

Special thanks to Mona Lisa for her contribution and beautiful Forward

Contents

Forward with The Mona Lisa .... Page 6

Introduction .... Page 11

Chapter 0. The Fool .... Page 16

Chapter 1. The Magician .... Page 22
Chapter 2. High Priestess .... Page 32
Chapter 3 The Empress .... Page 36
Chapter 4. The Emperor .... Page 42
Chapter 5. The Hierophant .... Page 50
Chapter 6. The Lovers .... Page 58
Chapter 7. The Chariot .... Page 66

Chapter 8. Strength .... Page 76
Chapter 9. The Hermit .... Page 84
Chapter 10. The Wheel of Fortune .... Page 92
Chapter 11. Justice .... Page 100
Chapter 12. The Hanged Man .... Page 106
Chapter 13. Death .... Page 112
Chapter 14. Temperance .... Page 118

Chapter 15. The Devil .... Page 126
Chapter 16. The Tower .... Page 132
Chapter 17. The Star .... Page 140
Chapter 18. The Moon .... Page 148
Chapter 19. The Sun .... Page 156
Chapter 20. Judgement .... Page 162
Chapter 21. The World .... Page 168

Chapter 22. The Mona Lisa .... Page 174

Forward with the Mona Lisa

If you thought the smile on my face looked good on the classic painting hanging in the Louvre museum you should have seen the smile on my face when Vincent asked me to do a Forward in his book!

I was thrilled to hear him say he finally had a complete set of conversations with all 22 Major Arcana. After 12 years of excuses he finally did it.

His first book *Genius of the Tarot - A Guide to Divination with the Tarot* started it all by having a heart-to-heart conversation with five of the Major Arcana. He put those visionary discussions in the last chapter. He thought of it as entertaining reading to end the book with and nothing to do with the main substance of his work. Something just for fun, a few laughs and maybe a hint of insight for you, the reader.

When that book was released in 2012 Kirkus Book Reviews gave his debut high praise! But more conversations were encouraged by friends and family.

He wrote *The Essential Tarot - Unlocking the Mystery* in 2015 and reserved the last chapter again for more Tarot card conversations along with myself as an extra feature.

When he asked me to be a guest in that book I told him I didn't think I could do it. I just didn't feel comfortable being associated with Tarot cards. I thought I would be too boring compared to the magical Tarot. I would put his readers to sleep.

But Vincent told me *"Lisa you are going to be fantastic! Don't worry about a thing. Trust me, I will take care of all the details."*

Well he was right. We had such fun and before you knew it the whole thing was over. He made me feel right at home. I felt like I knew him for years. He's just got that way about him.

People loved that book as well. Vincent continued to shed new light on using these cards and why they work so effectively.

But people still wanted more conversations.

Lastly in 2017 he wrote *"Radical Tarot - Breaking all the Rules"* and added several more conversations with the cards. Again putting them in the last chapter of the book. People loved it and said you should do all twenty two!

That was when I knew he would make a complete set of conversations with all the Majors someday. By that time most of the conversations were already done and he only had to add several more to make a complete set.

I really do feel you will enjoy these pages as you discover each card's unique personality and how they interact with Vincent. The book is magical, entertaining and has it's own unique humor.

But most important you will see another side to these 22 Major Arcana. What they're like behind the scenes. A new twist on how to see these curious cards and the personalities each one brings to the table as they visit with the author. Each conversation may also give you something to think about pertaining to your own life.

So here we are all together in 2023. Like one big happy family as we celebrate the release of this book.

I haven't seen any of them since I worked with Vincent in *The Essential Tarot - Unlocking the Mystery* in 2015. They keep telling me "Lisa you look great! You haven't changed a bit!" I tell them "That's because I'm a painting."

My talk with Vincent from Essential Tarot is placed at the very end of the book. We thought making it the final conversation would be a nice touch.

So here it is "Conversations with the Tarot - A Dialogue with each of the 22 Major Arcana."

Keep smiling readers. The fun is just starting.

~ Mona Lisa

Introduction

I've never felt I would be doing much with these conversations. It was never intended to be anything more than fluff. My books are all down to earth information regarding the Tarot. The conversations with Tarot cards was meant as an ice breaker. Almost like recess when you were a kid in school. It was meant as a playground chapter. Just a satire with a twist to give you something to think about. Light hearted and nothing serious.

My real work was unique and time tested in reading the Tarot and that was, and still is, the purpose of my work. The conversations were just something to show that I do have a playful side.

I didn't really think they would draw much interest. I was wrong. When *Genius of the Tarot* came out it seemed like that last chapter was an attention getter. I had that book endorsed by Rachel Pollack, Mary K. Greer and two leading authors on creative thinking techniques who immediately liked what I was talking about.

I wrote that book to talk about a ground breaking discovery I stumbled upon. The Tarot reading can now be seen for what it really is. A creative thinking technique and how this new info explains it's ability to see into the future. How it finds answers can now be explained for the first time in it's history! And this new information can now be verified in psychological studies!

Rachel Pollack didn't say much about that at all in her endorsement. But she loved the conversations! She said I made the Tarot come alive with my conversatons. Go figure! She liked the gabfest!

My friends and family also seemed to show a lot of interest in the conversations. They loved them. I thought OK that's fine.

Kirkus Book Reviews saw it all from a different angle. They said the book had a solid foundation along with fresh perspectives. Their review said the book was innovative, entertaining, multi textured and done in an easy going conversational tone. Kirkus ended their endorsement by saying *"A worthy edition to any Tarot library, likely to teach new tricks to even the most experienced reader."* No mention of the conversations at all!

I thought YESSSSSSS!
I felt good to see that they recognised what I was striving for in that book.

But I still kept hearing about those conversations from people I met.

My second book *The Essential Tarot - Unlocking the Mystery* delved even deeper into the creative thinking technique used in the Tarot bringing into the picture *Conceptual Blending!* The deeper I looked into the psychological studies the more of a connection I found.

Just on a hunch I decided to make the last chapter more conversations with the cards again. As I was writing that book people would be saying "Are you going have more conversations in this one too? I would say "Yes, they will be in there."

When the book came out I went to friends and family and gave them a copy. The first thing they would asked me was "Did you do more conversations?" I would say "Yes, last chapter just like before."
They would instantly turn right to the end of the book not even looking at the other chapters and start reading.

So sometimes it was nuts.

I would be thinking who cares about that! Read the rest of the book! It's all ground breaking material never seen before!

So now I had 5 conversations in my first book *Genius of the Tarot* and followed that with 4 more and the Mona Lisa in my second book *The Essential Tarot*. Yes... You heard right....The Mona Lisa.

By the time I wrote "*Radical Tarot - Breaking all the Rules*" I knew I had to have a last chapter of conversations again or people would get pissed off! In that book I put 7 conversations in that last chapter.

Like before everyone would go to that last chapter first.

I write about the Tarot because I have some new ways of understanding the cards that have never been seen before. On the other hand those conversations with the cards seem to keep tugging on everyone's coat tail wanting all the attention.

Arthur Waite was a leading authority on esoteric studies, prominent with the world order known as the Golden Dawn as well as other mystery schools and societies back then. But he will always be known for his (rectified) Tarot deck more than any of his deeper work.

The Rider Waite Tarot was something he didn't really give much thought to. It wasn't that important to him. Pamela Colman Smith was the artist he hired to render the cards images. Just a deck of cards to him. His metaphysical study was his real work.

Lewis Carroll was known as a leading professor/author on mathematics who taught at Oxford University in England. No one really seems to care about that. But everyone knows of his creation *Adventures of Alice in Wonderland* and his sequel *Through the Looking-Glass*. Something he put together just for fun as a gift to a special little girl named Alice.

On a smaller scale I wonder if my conversations with the Tarot is what I'll be known for instead of breaking open the centuries old mystery of why the Tarot works.

If I ask the cards they just say *"Hell I dunno. Why you askin me for? Don't worry about it. It's not that important Vincent."*

So they aren't any help.

But those Major Arcana do have some good conversations to share with you here. Some are funny. Some are insightful. All are entertaining in some way or another. (At least they seem to think so!) These conversations will also leave you with an insight into their energy not usually seen by others. You gotta know somebody to get inside. I can do that for you.

And if you ever do have the chance to tap one on the shoulder yourself some day and they don't respond right away just tell 'em you know Vince from Chicago. They will probably say *"Oh why didn't ya say so? How's he doin? Haven't seen him in awhile. Tell him don't be such a stranger."*

Let them know I'll be around. Just been busy with stuff. Ya know how it goes.

So now let this Mad Hatter take you down another rabbit hole to a place you've never been before. Down the alley and through the back door.

They're a good bunch! Let's go meet them all.

Chapter 0   The Fool

Road Trip

Sitting here late at night writing this chapter of my book. As I write, I think of *John Steinbeck's— Grapes of Wrath*. I must have read that book four times in my life. I just love his work. Always writing about drifters living on the edge of life. Someday I'm gonna take a trip down *RT 66* just like the *Okie's* did in that book. Pack up my *Wrangler* and just go. No time schedule. Don't know how long I'll be gone. Maybe a week. Maybe a summer. Maybe a year. Maybe the rest of my life.

Then I hear a voice say *"So when are we going Tom?"*

"What! Where did that come from!?" as I look around the room I see the Fool standing right there in my room!

"Hey! I wondered if you would ever drop by." I said

"Hell Tom I'm closer to ya than you think. Just you and me Tommy boy. Let's hit *RT 66*. Whaddya say? It's only a few blocks from here. Let's pack the car."

"What? No way. I got too much to do— besides this book's gotta get done. And why you keep calling me Tom? My name's Vince.
You cant just pack up and go. You gotta plan these things."

"Why?"He said looking kinda puzzled

"Whaddya mean why?"

"Just go Tom."

"Im not Tom!"

"OK OK Geez........Tom."

"And why would I take you along anyway?" I said

"Well you take me everywhere now don't you?" he asked.

"Along with all the others in that pack of cards.
You're always calling on me. I need a *vacation* Tom! Don't you wanna see Oklahoma City? The Heart of *RT 66*." He said as he looked out my window.

"Well yes I always wanted to go to Oklahoma City.
Just for that reason too. The heart of *RT 66*." I answered.

"Well instead of reading about it, lets go!
You're too involved with books Tom.
Reading books. Writing books. Collecting books.
Why don't you go out and experience these things instead of just reading about them. Now you're not only reading and collecting books, you're writing books! You're symptoms are becoming worse Tom. The next stage will be volunteering in a public library.
You're getting to be that age anyway. Ya know... a senior."

"Libraries are wonderful places." I said

"See it's already starting.
You're reading about lives instead of living one.
Lets hitch-hike there."

"Huh! Hell no. I'm not hitch-hiking anywhere.
You're nuts." I snapped back, shaking my head with disbelief.

"I bet you couldn't go to Oklahoma City without taking that silly little cell phone with you."

"Well it comes in handy." I said. "I can let people know where I am and stuff."

"No one cares where you are Tom!
What— you think you're someone special?"

"A Cell phone's an important thing today.
What if we needed assistance or something. Huh?"

"Whaddya got to drink around here Tommy boy?" He asked as he opened up my fridge. "Ah *Miller*. Want one?" As he popped the top on a can of beer.

"Yeah I guess yeah." He tossed me a beer across the room before I got the words out of my mouth.

"Geez!" barely catching the cold can.

"So when's this book gonna get finished?" he asked

"Not sure." I said as I took a swig of my beer." It's been a slow go lately. Just can't seem to get in the groove."

"Don't write if you're not in the groove Tom.
The book will be shitty if you do."

"My book won't be shitty." I said as I gave him a serious look.

"Gonna be a shitty book Tom."

"It ain't gonna be shitty!" I said as I wiped the beer from my mouth. "Ain't gonna be shitty — OK?"

"Maybe you need to go to Oklahoma to get some fresh ideas Tom. Ya know, get outta here for awhile. So you can avoid your book being so shitty."

"I said it ain't gonna be shitty!"

"Got a title yet Tom?" As he looks over my shoulder taking a slug of beer

"Yeah I got a title."

"It's probably a shitty title too." he said

"It ain't shitty!"

"What's the title Tom?"

"The Essential Tarot — Unlocking the Mystery" I said rather proudly..

"Shitty title Tom."

"No it aint! Ya know, maybe you should just go to Oklahoma your self if you're so damn smart." I said. "Go ahead if you think you wanna go there, go ahead. I don't need you in my deck."

"Tom's writing a book and its gonna be shitty" He sang as he danced back and forth in front of me doing an old soft shoe.
"Maybe you should change the title to— *My shitty book*" He said as he threw me another cold beer.

I popped the beer and just looked in disbelief at this Joker.

"Come on Tom lets go."

"Where Oklahoma?" I asked.

"Yes Oklahoma."

"You really wanna go there?" I asked again.

"No, you really wanna go there. But I'll tag along" He answered back.

"Ok, road trip, lets get going. Grab the beer outta the fridge." I said as I turned off my computer.

"Really?" He said.

"Hell yea, Lets do it. We'll be there by tomorrow afternoon. Maybe it will give me some ideas for the book if I get on the road."

"Yeah Tom! Now you're talkin!"

The two of us got in the *Wrangler* and headed for the expressway. 200 miles later I went for my cell phone. Damn! I forgot to grab it off the counter. Oh well— I lit a smoke and looked over at the passenger seat. There was nothing there but my deck of Tarot cards with the *Fool* card on top face up.

I looked at the deck and said *"Ain't gonna be a shitty book!"*

Chapter 1   The Magician

The Carni trickster

Yesterday I noticed a Ferris Wheel was setting up a few towns over. A carnival! Thinking about being a vendor there. I always liked carnivals. Being a part of that setting always works well for me when it happens.

They will usually let you set up somewhere out of the way - for a small fee of course. Something about a carnival that just feels bizarre to me.

Just got a magic in the air whenever you see that Ferris Wheel. I never get on the Ferris Wheel. Never have time. I want to do that some day. Something about that big wheel makes me think there's magic in the air.

Then I hear a voice behind me say "It is a magic place".

I turn around to see the Magician standing there looking over my shoulder at my computer screen. "Wow! Hi!"

"Hi back" he says to me. "You're thinking about setting up shop at a carnival aren't you?"

"Well yeah I was." I replied looking a little surprised

"You can still detect a slight sense of magic in the air walking the midway of a carnival today but most of that has disappeared." he said with a somber look on his face.

"What? No. I can still feel the magic of those places." I said

"Ha! You should have seen the old carnivals in action Vince. Nothing like that going on today."

"How so" I asked?

He looked out my window as he started to reminisce and said "All changed over the years. New regulations and such. And yes vendors like you would follow carnivals from one town to another and set up their tents to do business."

He looked over at my Tarot deck, flipped over the top card showing the 6 of Wands and continued. "Carnivals usually had a 6 month schedule all lined up each year so it was good for vendors who traveled with them. Those vendors were called *40 milers*. They would usually follow you for about 40 or 50 miles. They were locals and would fade out after awhile. Then head back home." he said with a slight smile.

He threw over another card showing the 5 of Swords and said "As long as they didn't have a scammer booth or a gyp joint cheating the customers. That would give the carnival a bad name. Usually that is something the *Patch* watched for all the time."

He turned and looked at me and said "If they were an honest booth the *Patch* wouldn't give them any trouble. If not, you were thrown out... literally!"

"What's a *Patch*?" I asked.

"The *Patch*?" he said with a smile " Oh he was the guy running things for the owners. The go-between for the town officials and the carnival. Making sure everybody is taken care of. You know what I mean. Police Chief, Mayor, things like that. If they benefit...so does the carnival."

"And if everything goes well the carnival could come back next year and do it again. If not ...well." He went on saying, "The *Patch* was like a manager. He made sure all was working well."

"The answer man for whatever comes up. He patched things up. And things would come up. Crooked vendors tagging along was one of those things."

He looked down at that 5 of Swords and said "Yes things have changed since those days."

"How so?" I asked.

"Oh jeez it's a whole different midway today."

"What's a midway?" I asked?

"The midway was about a mile long walkway of the whole carnival. Rides set up on both ends with shows, games and grab joints all lined up in the center." As he threw over another card, The Moon card, and pointed to the pathway between the two towers on that card.

"What's a Grab Joint?" I asked.

He threw over the 8 of Cups and said "It's a vendor booth that sells food. Usually has a grill for hamburgers. No where to sit, just grab the food and eat as you walk away. A Grab Joint." he said, pointing to the guy walking away in the 8 of Cups card.

"Yeah you had sword swallowers, escape artists, freak shows." he said turning over the 8 of Swords. "Hell I remember one booth at a carnival had an 80lb chimp you could wrestle. If you lasted just one minute with that chimp you won a prize." he said with a laugh.

"An 80 pound chimp couldn't be that hard to wrestle with for one minute. I weigh 195lbs." I said.

"No? That chimp would throw you around like a rag doll for sixty seconds Vincent! That would be fun to see ..... You in the ring with that chimp! Ha!"

"Carnivals used to be a lot more than a bunch of vendors offering the things they do today."

"Freak shows, the ever popular *Hooch* tent. Games and of course you had the Fortune Teller….like you Vincent. But you're the only thing that survived. Sitting in your tent with a big smile on your face as the people walk by" he said, looking at me as he turned over the 9 of Cups.

He continued "Today you just have vendors selling sunglasses, crafty stuff, maybe purses and other leather products like wallets. Some handmade shawls, hats and a whole lot of jewelry. It's all boring stuff today Vincent."

"What's a *Hooch* tent?" I asked.

"Beautiful exotic dancers who don't leave much to the imagination. Just enough to keep you coming back every night. Those tents were always packed full of dirty old men. Ya know….guys like you." he said with a laugh as he turned over another card. The World card.

"Usually the tent name will be big bold letters saying something like G-String Review starring…The Radiant Miss Reynolds or some name like that." he went on as he pointed to the dancing woman in the center of that World card.

"I'm not a dirty old man." I said looking down at that card.

"You are old aren't you Vincent?"

"Well yeah I guess. I'm 70."

"Yeah 70 is old Vincent.
Did you take a shower yet this morning?" he asked

"No, not yet" I said.

"Well then you're a dirty old man right?"

"Oh please." I said as I drank my coffee.

"And if you don't get a haircut soon you could be in the damn freak show. Freak shows were big draws too." he said with a laugh.

"Yes but that was kinda cruel wouldn't you say? Freak shows?" I asked.

"Not at all Vincent."

"A traveling carnival sees some poor soul who was born a midget or with some unusual defect living on a farm somewhere with their family, just being a burden to them." he says as he throws over the Wheel of Fortune card and points to the freaky characters clinging to the wheel on that card.

He gave that Wheel card a spin on my table and said "Then the freak gets a chance to travel with the carnival and make some money to send back home. And they made a good living doing that. Gave them a sense of pride."

As the spinning of that card on my table slowed down he continued, "The more of a freak you were, the more money you made! Conjoined twins at birth better known as Siamese Twins, Bearded lady. Fat man, Tiny man. They were accepted and made friends with all the others working the carnival."

"I remember one man born with three legs." he continued as the spinning card came to a dead stop,

"A carnival picked him up somewhere in Iowa. All he had to do was sit there in a chair showing he had three legs. Oh he would stand up now and then. Ya know…to stretch his legs…all three of them."

"But he made good money and he felt for the first time a sense of belonging to something. He made friends and became part of the family."

"Made friends?" I said.

"Sure. You're part of a carnival. You're part of a family. "

"And the gaffers running those carni booths were real pros." he went on

How so?" I asked.

"You take your date to the carnival and while walking the midway you hear a loud voice coming from one booth. You stop and notice some young scrawny guy sitting in a basket above a tank of water yelling insults at you."

"You hear his loud voice calling you a dork and telling your date how pretty she is and what is she doing with a dork like you. Tempting you to buy three balls and try to hit the target that puts him in the tank of water below."

"Do you take the bait? Are you a *mark*? The scrawny carni sitting in that basket keeps an eye out for guys like you all night. And he finds them."

"A *mark* will stop and buy three balls. As he throw the balls one at a time you hear that scrawny carni saying how he throws like a girl. Calling him a wimp. Shouting to all the people walking by to look at this wimp throwing the balls at me. What a wimp!"

"By the time that boy is done, the *mark* bought 75 balls before he finally hit the target and dumped him in the drink below. That's a carni at work." he said as he snapped his fingers.

"Whaddya mean a *mark*" I asked

"A target, a sucker. Like a cocky young guy wanting to show off to his pretty date at the carnival." he said with a sly grin.

"And let's not forget the Fortune Teller booth? That's your line Vincent!"

"Well yeah I guess you could say that."

"Abdule the Amazing! For just a $5 ticket he will guess your birth month within two months. Test his powers and if you fool him you can choose from any of the merchandise behind him hanging on the wall!"

"You look and see cameras, watches, dolls and all sorts of interesting stuff on that wall! All looks like each is worth about $20!"

"Sounds like a good chance to get something for nothing. How's a booth like that gonna make money?" I asked

"OK. Well there are 12 months in the year, right?"

"Yeah." I replied.

"And he will guess your birth month and will not be off by more than 2 months right?."

"OK, yeah." I said

"Which really means five months." he said, holding out all five fingers.

"Five months! You said only 2 months not 5!" I said.

"Same thing." he replied with a wave of his hand.

"How so?" I asked.

"Well let's say you were born in January."

"OK, continue." I replied.

"That means if he guesses February or March…that's within 2 months right?"   "Yes." I said.

"Or if he guesses November or December that is within 2 months too. Right? So that adds up to 5 months total. Nov. Dec, Jan, Feb, March."

He continued and threw over the 7 of Swords,
"And as you come up on stage for him to get a " psychic vibration" of your birth month he quickly looks you over for any jewelry you're wearing too."

"Maybe you're wearing pearls let's say or a moonstone. Those are the stones a Gemini might wear. If you're wearing a garnet there's a good chance you're a Capricorn."

He pointed to the sneeky character stealing swords from the enemy camp in that 7 of Swords card and says "If you do stump the Amazing Abdule, the stuff on the wall to choose from is all cheap imitation products and nothing worth more than around $5 anyway so the booth breaks even on you. "

"Is he psychic at all?" I asked.

"No, just a carni with a turban on his head. His real name was Sam. Used to be a radio repairman from Detroit."

"Today the midway just has some simple games and vendors selling their wares. Tee shirts, sun glasses, hats, trinkets, gifts, crafts, engraved beer mugs. It's endless what you see for sale there. All boring junk." he said.

He went on saying "Thrill rides or taking a chance to win something for nothing. You could find so much at those old carnivals. Stuff you won't see anywhere today."

He went on as he turned over the Devil card! "You would find a fascinating world where you might meet a midget or a three eyed man, con-artists and pimps, drug addicts and other strange types all getting along together. It had a code of ethics all it's own."

He continued, "It's a world that is never really surprised at anything. Like a dream world…anything goes! From thieves to solid citizens."

"Whores to housewives, natures monsters and ordinary Homosapiens. Their lives don't always run smoothly but neither do those on the outside world. That's just life."

"Well that carnival energy is mostly all gone today Vincent. But people still go as if they are searching for that magic to come back to life again. As if they know what a real carnival is supposed to be like."

"Don't let me discourage you Vincent. There still is a magic about walking through a carnival's midway. Make your booth be part of that magic. That's your power Vincent. Use it!"

I looked down at the cards he threw over on my table, and when I looked back up the room was empty. Then something blows across my floor.

I got up to grab it. A small piece of red paper. A ticket. It reads " $10. Admit One Ride"

Thanks Magician! I think I see carnivals in a different way now. I'm gonna take the time to get on that Ferris Wheel this year. Then I'll return back to my booth and bring some magic to some happy people.

I have a feeling a good Tarot reader can still fill a carnival with magic today if he tries.

I'll find out soon enough.

Chapter 2   The High Priestess

~ Mystery ~

I sat at my desk ready to write. The room was silent except for the ticking of the clock. The candle fluttered in the dimly lit room and the smoke of incense sorta danced with the flame. I started my chapter on the High Priestess, and just the thought of that card made me wonder about much: the mysterious High Priestess. As I looked at that card, I thought that she is one of the most popular cards in the tarot, for sure. Yes, queen of the hop!

Then I heard a voice say, "Thank you."

What? Who said *Thank you?*

Then I heard it again: "Thank you."

I looked at my deck and there on the top was the High Priestess with a smile coming across her face. She was beautiful sitting there dressed in her flowing, blue gown and wearing that crescent-moon headdress.

"Wow!" I said as I gave a blank stare at the card addressing me. "I never expected you to come forth. Other cards, maybe yes, but you! The High Priestess? I'm honored. Please excuse the mess." I tried in vain to straighten up my desk area.

"You don't have to make such a fuss," she said. "I know much about you. More than you realize. More than you know about yourself." She smirked.

"Oh. Well, yes, I guess you would. It's just I didn't take a shower yet or shave or nothin', and I would have if I knew you were going to visit me." I tried to straighten my hair out a little bit and sit straighter as I adjusted my chair.

"Oh, nonsense!" she said as she waved her hand in the air as if to swipe my words away. "So, what are you going to write about me?"

"Well, I'm not sure yet. I was going to sit here and just see what comes to me. You know, sorta intuitive-like. That's what you're all about, anyway, so I figured that would be a good approach. You know, being the High Priestess and all."

"Good idea," she said as she leaned forward, looking into my computer screen. "Just let things flow, I always say."

"I think you are gonna be the hardest for me to write about, though. I always sorta favored you over the others," I said, trying not to sound too silly.

"Well, I'm flattered. So you think of me how, then?" She smiled as she gave me a flirtatious glance. "Unattainable? Mysterious? After all, I am the virgin," she said with a smile.

"I'm not sure why I feel that way about you, actually, but I do. Never cared about the virgin thing, really. You're just special."

"Oh, yes you do, my dear. You see, the fact that I am mysterious is what makes you feel that way. The unattainable High Priestess makes you want to attain me all the more. But if you did attain me, then that power would be destroyed for ever. My essence is mystery. Once mystery is known, it is no longer a mystery. That's the paradox of it. I am mystery. So you see, in order for me to exist, you must never attain me in any way, shape, or form. For, once you do, my essence will be gone."

"So the virgin things stands for more than just a sexual energy?" I said.

"Sure it does, Vincent. It stands for the mystery and wonder of things. The unknown. That has a real power in itself, mystery does. Although mankind has really exploited the sexual thing to an extreme. And let's not forget getting tossed into a volcano every now and then."

"How so? The sexual thing, I mean."

"'How?' you say? Man has always been fascinated with all the sexuality of woman. Women give birth, women have breasts, women have menstrual cycles. Women have multiple orgasms! Let's face it: women have a lot more sexual vibration than men do. And if men cannot have or experience all of that sexuality, then the next best thing is to own it. And men have owned women for centuries."

"I agree." I said "But that is changing now. Don't you think?"

"About time, wouldn't you say?" she answered.

"So let me get this straight. If I want you in some manner in my life, and I get that, then I destroy the very thing I wanted about you. Therefore, the only way to keep your essence is to leave you alone?"

"You got it. So here I sit," she said.

"Any regrets?" I gave her a curious look.

"You'll never know," she said.

"Gee, I really think you're something. Can I call you sometime?"

"You know where to find me," she answered as I heard her voice drift away.

"Hey! Wait a minute! Hey! I think I'm in love! No, really! Don't go yet! Damn—I'm in love with a damn tarot card!

"That's it! Oh well, story of my life. Always looking for my soul mate, and she's always just out of reach. Time to get to bed." I crushed out my smoke and finished the last of my glass of wine, got in bed, and turned off the light.

As I lay there, dozing in and out of sleep, I felt a gentle breeze around my face, followed by the wisp of fine cloth brushing against my cheek. As I realized this experience to be more than a dream, a soft hand touched my cheek, and then the soft voice of that mystery woman whispered into my ear: "I will always be here in your heart."

Then I felt a kiss on my cheek. "I am everywhere and in a thousand faces. Your book might take some aspects of mystery out of the tarot, which means it takes some mystery out of me." was the last thing I remembered hearing before drifting off into sleep.

Chapter 3   The Empress

~ The Mother ~

"Good morning, Vin. Coffee?"

"Wha—? Looking at the clock, it said 6:00 a.m. I guess I should get up anyway.

"Coffee, Vin?"

"What? Who said *coffee?* Who's here? Only my mother calls me Vin. Ma?"

"Over here, sleepy head."

There was my tarot deck next to a cup of fresh coffee steaming away on the night stand. I stared at it, trying to wake up and figure out what the hell was going on here. As I gathered my thoughts, I noticed the top card of my deck was face up. It was the Empress, and she had a big smile on her face!

"Now you're awake," she said. "I made the coffee just like you like it. Only three scoops, and the rest of the pot is poured into your thermos on the counter. I washed your cup out too. It was filthy."

"Thought it looked different" I said, staring at the clean cup. What's on your mind?" I said as I grabbed my robe.

"You needed a visit," she sighed as she gently patted my forearm. "I noticed you're doing well, and I thought you needed to be reminded of that."

"I am?".

"Yes, you are doing exactly as you wanted to do. You have most everything you sought to get out of life, Vin."

"I do, huh? Well, where the hell is it all, then?"

"Look around you, Vin. What are the things you want? What are the things you have? Anything missing?"

"I can use some things," I said as I looked around the room.

"Yes everyone can use some more 'things,' but do they need them, and at what price do you pay to acquire those things anyway? You have to scurry around hustling to be at places you don't want to be, doing things you don't want to do. That's the price you pay for those things' you think you can use. Is it worth it? What are your plans for today, Vin?"

"I don't really know yet." I yawned, with the coffee waiting at my mouth for the chance to enter. "Probably some phone readings and work on my book some, A few clients at the coffee house this afternoon."

"Ooooh, poor deprived boy you are. Ooooh. You pay your bills every month, you have food in the fridge, a few dollars in your wallet, a car, and a phone. What are you missing? You have your health, even though I wish you would quit smoking those darn cigarettes. Not to mention the drinking."

"I bought a pipe, and I'm cutting down. I don't know; I just feel like I should have more. Most people do at my age, ya know."

"Most people at your age don't have something you do have that is golden."

"Oh, and what's that?" I asked.

"Happiness. They are controlled and manipulated, and their time is not theirs. Yes, they have money in the bank that they probably will never use. They have a shiny new car, a big house with a manicured lawn, nice expensive furniture that they try not to scratch, and nice new clothes that don't feel any more comfortable than your old clothes feel. Don't you see what you acquired? The ability not to need and still be happy and feel secure. You live a life without luxury and riches, but you're happy. You might not realize it, but you feel more secure than a lot of the people who have all that other stuff, including money in the bank. It's funny, but the more people have, the less secure they feel. Drink your coffee, it's getting cold."

"OK, I'm drinking it."

"Your livelihood is a card reader. That's a big accomplishment."

"It is? Well, where's all the money, if it's such a big accomplishment?"

"Who said anything about money? You're confusing money with actual wealth.

"There is no established system to do what you do—no unions or ads in the paper saying, 'tarot reader wanted.' Isn't that what you always wanted? To be a reader and not part of the system? You always hated the system anyway. Nine to five and all that. But that is the game most people want to play. Bless them, and hope that they are happy. They did what they wanted, and you have too. You are rich in your own way, Vin. You have all the things you wanted to have, and you stopped spending time trying to get things you thought you were supposed to want, things you didn't really want but felt you were expected to try to get: married with children, house in the 'burbs, full-time job, traffic jams, church on Sunday morning, BBQ on weekends, and watching the game on TV after you cut the grass. That is not you, Vin! Yes, you tried it. You didn't like it, so you took a different path. Your own path. And your path was reading tarot cards.

"How many decks do you have in here right now" she said as she looked around the room.

I noticed the deck on the shelf and one on my desk. "Two decks," I said.

"Ahah," she said. "What about in that black box over there?"

"Oh yeah, two more decks in there too."

"And how about this deck here on the shelf?"

"Oh, yeah, forgot that one."

"So—five decks of tarot cards in a one-room studio apartment."

"Well, to be honest, I have about ten more decks in that big trunk there that I use as a coffee table."

"Where else do you have them, Vin? Fess up."

"Well, I'm not hiding them, for cryin' out loud! Jeez, you're acting like my mother now."

"Well, I am the Empress, and I do live in every mother, so that would make sense. Where else? Come on, now."

"OK, let's see: one deck in my jeep. No, two decks in my jeep. Lynda's kitchen, top of the fridge. Hell, I don't exactly know how many decks I have hanging around here! A lot of them."

"And you use them too, don't you?"

"Yes, I use them. That's my bread and butter."

"Exactly!" she said as she poured me more coffee. "So you see, you're successful.

You want me to make you some waffles?"

What? No ma'am, I mean Empress," I said as I lit another cigarette. "Waffles! Ha!"

"You should eat."

"I know." I nodded. "I want to tell you that I appreciate you reminding me of where I'm at and how I'm doing. It helps, and I guess we should all stop and count our blessings from time to time. But right now I have to get changed and run some errands."

"Not before you finish your waffles. They're on the counter in the kitchen."

"But I don't want any waffles!"

"Eat your waffles, ….. and don't slouch!"

"I'm not eating waffles—like I said, I got things to do. What you gonna do about it? Ground me? Ha!"

"Well, good luck finding your car keys till that plate is clean."

"Hey! What'd you do with my keys!"

"Have a good day, son. I'll check in on you later."

"Yeah, that's what I'm afraid of!" I said with a mouthful of waffles. "Ya know what! This talk with you is scarier than the talk I had with that Devil card!"

Chapter 4 The Emperor

Accomplishments?

Sitting here at my table thinking about how I got through another year. It went OK. Got some things accomplished. A number of lectures, classes and many readings for clients as well. I have come up with some great ideas for a few more books and now I just have to get them started.

Yes, a good year. It's funny but sometimes I feel that my journey is still just starting, even after this long. But I'm enjoying it just the same.

Then I hear someone say "You enjoy going around in circles?"

I turn and see the Emperor sitting across the room looking at me.

"Well hello."

"Hello back." he says
 "I asked if you enjoy going around in circles."

"What do you mean?" I asked

"Well you're sitting here pondering all of your wonderful accomplishments this year and I have to laugh. You haven't done anything that exceptional. You threw a few cards and made a few bucks. That some big deal to you Vincent?"

"Yeah." I answered. "I made it through another year as a Tarot reader. That's my profession."

"Profession? You're a struggling soul in an obscure enterprise my friend. A craft, not a profession. A street craft I might add. That's gonna be your legacy? Not too impressive Vincent."

"Fancy words, Obscure Enterprise" It's not an obscure enterprise. It's a unique craft and it's been around a long time. I counsel and I'm good at what I do. I'm one of the best!" I said

"Oh? So that's a big deal then? Being a card reader? Better than the rest? What have you done so different than others in your craft?"

"Well there's some people out there that feel I know the Tarot cards better than most other readers do." I said.

"So you know all about Tarot cards. You think that's all you need to do?
That's like saying Stephen King become a great author by knowing all about the type of pencil he wrote his novels with. Tarot cards are just a tool Vincent. A tool for the successful reader. Are you a big name with the Tarot cards Vincent?"

"I get by."

"You're a typical reader, that's all. No great shake."

"TYPICAL!" I yelled. "I'm far from typical pal. I feel I'm the best there is in my craft. The best! I'd put myself up against any other reader – card for card!"

"And where has that gotten you Vincent?
Many ideas go through your head every day and you just sit on them. Manifest those ideas into a reality!
Create them. Make them real – not fantasy."

"Is that your power then?" I asked. "Turning ideas into realities?
A builder of realities?"

"Yes, that's me Vincent."

"Well why don't you manifest my apartment getting cleaned Mr. Big Shot Emperor instead of telling me what I'm doing wrong."

"I wouldn't waste my time Vincent
I got better things to do and so should you.
Act on your ideas. Get off your butt. Although this place does look like a train wreck." he said , looking around my apartment.

"People walk around with great ideas going through their minds all the time. They just don't act of them. So what good is an idea if it just stays in your head Vincent? Turn it into a reality. People are too afraid it might fail. So they play it safe and don't do anything with their ideas or their dreams."

"Failure terrorizes people and it shouldn't. That's what makes the difference between a winner and a loser. Fear of failure. Whoever invented the sailing ship also invented the shipwreck." he said, pointing a finger at me. "Failure is all part of the game and you're in the midst of it right now. Keep on going!"

"Its easy for you to say, sure. You're the Emperor. That's what you do. Make things happen. You turn ideas into realities. I mean you are the energy behind great accomplishments. Things like the United Nations, Mathematics. Technology, Science. The compass. Even the wheel!.."

"Yes, that's true" He said smugly looking at himself in my mirror. "The wheel was really big wasn't it?
But not everything has to be of such magnitude. There are personal accomplishments as well Vincent."

"Well I'm trying to write another book your majesty. What do I call you anyway?"

"Your majesty sounds good to me Vincent. I like that. And kneeling before me – looking at the floor as you speak would be kinda cool to see you do too."

"Yeah you would. Mr. Big Shot. Don't hold your breath."

He just grinned.
" I am pretty good aren't I Vincent."

"Well how come you're not helping me then?" I asked

"I do help you every day Vincent. I'm that haunt inside of you that says keep going with your ideas.
That's me pestering you."

"Oh, is that what that irritating sensation in my mind is?"

"Yes. Yours truly."

"Well why don't you manifest some TV shows for me to be on. Why don't you manifest some big agent calling me on the phone right now, wanting a contract with me? Huh? Mr Big Shot Emperor? I don't hear the phone ringing Mr. Big Shot Emperor.
See that lump of plastic over there on the coffee table? That's called a telephone. Is it ringing? No!"

"What, you want me to hold your hand through the whole thing. Hand it to you on a silver platter?" he said with a smile.

"If I did that you wouldn't feel the gratification of accomplishment. You need to manifest that yourself. It's up to you to take the initiative my friend. Network. Get out there and let people know who you are. Interaction is key Vincent. I just plant the seeds in your mind."

"Yeah well you plant a lot of weeds in my mind too.
Why don't you plant some money in my wallet while your so busy planting."

"OOOHHHH. Poor wittle vincy wincy is twying to whyte his wittle boook."

"Papus wrote Tarot of the Bohemians in 1889. He didn't have access to information that you have today. Same with Levi, Case, Waite, Crowley and the rest Vincent. They didn't even have cars to get around in."

"They didn't have the internet to find information with. You want perks? They had to saddle a horse just to get to the library. Living in this time in history you have all sorts of perks around you. If an opportunity knocked on your door and said "Hello, I'm an opportunity." You would say NOT INTERESTED. and slam the door in its' face!"

"Besides. I give you some perks here and there. A corporate party, new clients. Even helped get you started with your books."

"You had nothing to do with my books." I said.

"Are you sure about that Vincent? I create opportunities don't I?"

"Well yeah, I guess so."

"It's up to you to grab them when they come. If you're bright enough that is."

"I'm bright enough! You think you're some big deal Mr. Emperor. Well I don't need you!"

"Show me Vincent!"

"I'll show you alright! They'll be naming a street after me when I'm done!"

"Now your talkin Vincent!
Show me and I might even be tempted to throw some more perks your way. If I feel its promising that is."

"This year's gonna be spectacular! YOU WATCH ME PAL!"

"I will be. You can bet on that." he answered

"Now I got work to do. I can't be sitting here wasting my time talking to you, Mr. Big Shot Emperor."

"Good. We will see. And I'll be watching." he said as he walked out my door.

I closed the door behind him and thought... "I got important things to do around here. Like how am I gonna market this book? I'll get the break I'm looking for and I'll be ready for it when it comes too."

Then I hear '*rrring....rrring.....rrring.*'
Oh, that lump of plastic on the coffee table is making a noise again. I picked up the phone and said....*"Hello?"*

Chapter 5   The Hierophant

Adjustments

I came across an old photo album in my dresser undernealth a bunch of things I will never use and have totally forgotten about. Ya know how drawers collect stuff like that. *"Don't know what to do with this...I'll just throw it in the drawer and forget about it."* That kinda stuff.

Looking through that old photo album I came across some pictures of my kid brother. I thought about how we were arguing when he passed. Never got a chance to resolve anything with him. Wish I woulda done more about that. Thought about that when he was laying there on his death bed ..... kinda late then I guess. The doctors said it was just a matter of time now. So we wait until he passes.

Our mother didn't really care to stick around. She signed some hospital papers the nurse brought in and then she wanted me to take her home. I looked at my brother one last time, grabbed his hand, and said "Good bye, good knowin ya bro!" and we walked out. But Lynda said "I'm gonna stay here with him." I'm glad Lynda stayed with him in his hour of need. He always liked Lynda. She's just got that way about her.

Lynda stayed by his bedside until he passed. That was four hours later. She just sat there talking with him and singing to him as if they were just visiting.

When he passed Lynda said the whole room started to smell like whiskey! She called the nurse into the room and said "He's gone." pointing to the flat lined ventilator. Then she said to the nurse "Do you smell that? Smells like whiskey in here." The nurse didn't smell anything unusual and said "No I don't smell anything."

Lynda knew it was a sign from him. She always gave my brother a fifth of Jameson Scotch Whiskey every year for his birthday. That was his favorite. Jameson Scotch Whiskey. That smell of whiskey filling the room the minute he passed was my brothers way of telling Lynda thanks for staying here with me to the end.

Leave it to him to pull that off. The minute he passed he's already sending Lynda signs. He had style!

I feel kinda bad I didn't square things up with him before he was gone. We were arguing about something stupid and I got a little out of line with him. I guess I'll just have to live with that now.

Then I hear someone say "We don't do enough in our living years for the ones we love."

I turn around and see the Hierophant standing behind me!
"OMG! Well hello to you .....sir. I mean .....Hierophant sir ... I mean ...."

He interrupted my stumbling words and said
"You can just address me as Father seeing you were baptized Catholic Vincent. That is how your consciousness sees me."

"How do you mean my consciousness Father?"

"Well you see a higher power through your perception of things. If you were Hindu, Muslim, Jewish or some other religion you would see me through that lens. It really makes no difference son. As long as you see me. That's what's important. Catholic works fine."

"OK but don't you feel all these different religions confuse everything? All these rules and customs differ with each religion." I asked.

"Some day it might only be one religion. But in the meantime religions do evolve as society evolves." said the Hierophant.

"How so Father." I asked.

"Religions are mankind's way of interpreting what God is. Mankind evolves and religions follow. As time goes on we make adjustments in the way we understand and practice each religion. We makes adjustments to the thinking at that time in history." said the Hierophant.

"Really? How so?" I asked

"Look at your Tarot cards Vincent. They used to be considered a dark force. Even sinful. Not so anymore. Just a deck of cards now.
It's what people do with them that can be dangerous. But for the most part they don't create a threat. People are just having fun with them."

"Well I'm glad you feel that way seeing I'm a full blown Tarot reader."

"I do Vincent. I do."

"But that's just about the cards Father. What about all the major stuff in religions? Has any of that changed?" I said.

"Of course it has. Look back in history."

Can you give an example?" I asked.

He looked at me as if trying to recall and said
"In 1095 Pope Urban II saw an opportunity to strengthen the Holy Roman Catholic Church. He held an historic council at Clermont in south-central France. He summoned French bishops and representatives of the faith from across Europe. There, outside of the cathedral in the open air he stirred the crowd with an eloquence that started the Holy Crusades which lasted over 250 years."

Oh yeah? What did he say?

The Hierophant thought for a minute and then spoke.

"Pope Urban's speech went like this Vincent" he said as he turned and circled back toward me and started.

Jerusalem is the navel of the world, a land which is more fruitful than any other, a land which is like another paradise of delights. This is the land which the Redeemner of mankind illuminated by his coming, adorned by his life, consecrated by his passion, redeemed by his death, and sealed by his burial. This royal city, situated in the middle of the world, is now held captive by his ememies and is made a servant, by those who know not God, for the ceremonies of the heathen. It looks and hopes for freedom; it begs unceasingly that you will come to its aid. It looks for help from you, especially, because God has bestowed glory in arms upon you more than on any other nation. Undertake this journey, therefore, for the remission of your sins, with the assurance of "glory which cannot fade" in the kingdom of heaven.

"That was on November 18, 1095 and started the symbol of the white cross and the battle cry *"God wills it!"* The Holy Crusade was born.

"Wow you know a lotta stuff." I said as I sat there glued to his words. "Can you tell me another example?" I asked

He looked at me and continued.

"Pope Innocent VIII issued one of the key documents in the history of witchcraft. The papal bill of December 5, 1484. It served as a justification for pitiless persecution. It was put in place to combat the Devil and save mankind from his clutches. This bill really opened up free reign for brutality such as the Spanish Inquisition which lasted for three centuries."

He smiled and said "Mankind would not tolerate that type of behavior in Gods name today. As we evolve so do our religions."

"Wow you know a lotta stuff." I said again.
"Maybe I should go the church now and then. Wouldn't hurt...I guess."

"Religions are meant to bring peace Vincent. A sense of belonging to something bigger than ourselves. A reminder that we are good and a part of something wonderful even if it is unexplainable at times."

"The cruelty that has come in the name of God was not the religion's fault. That's mankinds twisted way of understanding their religion's message."

"Mankind still needs guidance. A feeling of being at peace. When you feel troubled religion can give you a spiritual *pat on the back*. Maybe some suggestions. Advice. Counsel. Since its' beginning mankind has always sought the connection to a higher power. The Hierophant can give guidance. Bring peace of mind, even comfort. That is what we do for troubled souls."

I just sat that and stared at him in silence.

"You were looking at that photo album when I came in Vincent and you seemed troubled."

"Yeah wish I would have squared things up with my brother before he died. We were arguing." I said as I held the photo album.

"Well Vincent I can tell you that your brother is not disappointed with you or sad. He is in paradise now. He also has perfect awareness of everything including the universe itself.
 He knows how you feel Vincent. He also forgives you and he loves you. "

I listened closely to his words as I rubbed my eyes hard with the palms of my hands.Ya know...to smash the moisture to the other side of my eyeballs. Then I quickly put my hands on my knees and said "Thank you for telling me that Father. Makes me feel better."

"That is what I do Vincent. Bring peace of mind to those who need comfort."

"Stay well my son." he said as he extended out his hands in a blessing gesture.

When he walked out the door I thought maybe I should take another look at that Bible. Might be missing something. Beautiful mythology? Maybe I should reevaluate my thinking about all this stuff.

What a nice man. I picked out my Bible from the book shelf and thought "Thanks for the guidance Mr. Hierophant."

Then I thought of my brother and said " Hope you're enjoying paradise little brother! See ya when I get there!"

Chapter 6   The Lover

Ain't dat right darlin?

Out in my hallway I hear some man and a woman having a conversation.

"This is a bad idea"

"No it's not. Be quiet"

"I think you're wrong but then again what else is new."

"I'm not wrong and shut up will ya. For pete sake Hoobie will ya comb your damn hair please. He's gonna think you're a slob or somethin."

"I'm not a slob! I'm comfortable. Is that a crime?"

"Oh so the slob is comfortable. Well at least your comfortable....slob!"

"Oh– and you're an oil painting? Look in the mirror will ya."

"Schh! This is it! His apartment. Knock on the door."

"You knock on the door. You're the one who wanted to come here."

"Schhhh." *Knock Knock...Knock Knock*

Damn! "WHO'S THERE?" I yell through the door.

— *Knock Knock...Knock Knock*

"OK Ok" I said as I open the door. I see an old couple standing there. A short stocky old woman with curly gray hair wearing blue jeans, sneakers and a white tee shirt and a tall skinny old guy with wispy white hair wearing an old pair of black khakis, work shoes and a wrinkled, striped shirt, buttoned crooked so that the right side is higher than the left by two buttons.

I say "Hello–Can I help you?"

"Yeah" she says as she walks in and looks around my room. He follows and says "hi".

Then she says "See? What did I tell ya? I told ya didn't I? See?"

He just nods in agreement and I say "What? Who are you two? and what you doing in my place?"

She looks at him and says "See? He doesn't know who we is. I told you he wouldn't know."

"Know what?" I said "Who the hell are you guys!"

"Come on Vince. Guess. Come on." she says.

"I don't know you." I answered.

"Need a hint?" she says as she rest her head on his shoulder and bats her eyes showing a big grin. He just stands there looking bored as he looks around my room.

"I need you two to get outta here!"

"See Hoobie Hon?, I told you he wouldn't know who we was. He's no Tarot card reader." She says, resting her head on his shoulder.

"Wait a minute! Who comes into my place and says I don't know the cards!"

"Sandy that's who" she says with a smile showing a few crooked teeth.

"He doesn't know those tarot cards Hoobie hon."
He just laughs and as he grins his false teeth drop a little outta place.

"Who are you two!"

"We's the Lovers Vince! The Lovvveeeers.
Ain't dat right Hoobie honey?" she says as she puts her arm around his waist and gives him a squeeze.

"What!!! The Lovers!! You mean like from the Tarot cards Lovers?!!!"

"That's right Vince..That is us." she says.

"You mean number Six....of the Major Arcana...The Lovers....."

"He seems surprised Hoobie hon."

"He just grins and laughs some more as he nods his head looking around my room."

"But you can't be the Lovers!! You two are really old...and really ug–.....You two are really old."

"That's right Vince, we is really old and we still loves each other too. Ain't dat right Hoobie darlin?"

"uuuu yeah", he mumbles out a small laugh as he nods his head.

"But the lovers are young!"

"Not always Vince. You can still be in love when you is old too Vince. Ain't dat right Hoobie?"

"eh yeah. When are we going for Chinese?" he said "You said we were just gonna stop here for a minute. It's way past a minute. Let's go. OK?." he continued

"Will ya shut up Hoob! We just got here for chriss sake."

"I'm hungry lets get Chinese like we said we would."

"Hoob does your brain work at all? All morning that's all you think of is eating Chinese. You get the same damn thing every time. Egg Fu Yung."

"Vince that's all he ever gets every time we go eat Chinese. Egg Fu Yung."

"Hoobie. Wanna try some pot stickers?
No...I want Egg Fu Yung."

"What's a matter with Egg Fu Yung?" he asked

"He has no brains Vince."

"I got brains. You don't have any brains." he said.

"Where you keep your brains Hoobie? In your butt? They ain't in your head, that's for sure. Take your brains out of your butt and put them back in your head where they belong Hoobie."

"Oh the profound scientist has spoken" he says

"Why do I put up with this Vince?" Ya know when I was young, I coulda married a doctor. His name was Frank. And he was so cute too. But I decided to marry Mr.Egg Fu Yung over here."

"I think that doctor's name was Frankenstein, not Frank. And he created you. Ha Ha" he said.

"You see what I have to put up with Vince? A brainless egg fu young eating butt head. Vince his brain never matured to full size."

"Oh, the mummy speaks!" he said

"OK, I need you two to settle down." I said

"You see what you started Hoobie? You got Vince all upset. You're so ignorant. He's just ignorant Vince. He can't help it."

"Well you're the one who wanted to barge in and bother this guy. Just like you bother everyone else you comes in contact with." he says

"How do I bother anyone?"

"You open your big mouth. That's how you bother everyone. You open up your big mouth and suck all the oxygen out of the room every time you inhale with your big mouth."

"OK, you two just settle down for a minute will ya?
You two are supposed to be the lovers right? Old ones but the lovers just the same. How long have you two been together?" I asked

"Long time." she says and he just nods in agreement.

"I wanted to tell you both I appreciate you coming by and helping me with the Lovers Tarot card. You two have seen much of life together and have faced it all side by side for many years. That's something to be proud of. Nothing to do with wealth or living fancy. It's just living it out together and you two did that. Two souls that decided to go through this thing we call life, hand in hand."

They both look in opposite directions from each other in silence.

"Be proud of your bond together. Now give each other a hug. OK?"

She and he both turn to each other. He looks down at her and she peeks up at him.

"Come on now you two. Make up." I said

Then she says "I'm sorry Hoobie."

He says "I'm sorry Sandy" Then he kisses her on the check and she hugs him close to her and rest her head on his chest.

"There! I'm glad to see the Lovers back on track here."

"Now why don't you two go out and get some Chinese food. Egg Fu Yung sound good Hoob?" I asked

"Yeah." he says

I open my door and say "Thanks for the visit. See ya. Bye."

As they walk down the hall I hear her say. "I'm gonna get some pot stickers. You wanna try a pot sticker Hoobie?"

"Naw, ...Egg Fu Young for me."

"OK – Just a thought." she says.

"Dat Vincent was a nice man Hoobie." she says

"Yeah I guess." he says

Chapter 7   The Chariot

1966 GTO

I have always associated the Chariot to Confidence. Moving forward without doubt.
 So sure and so adept that it cannot be stopped from moving forward on it's objective. An unstoppable force.

That's when I hear a knock on my door. I open my door and there stands the Charioteer!
 He walks in without any hesitation and says "I got here as quickly as I could."

"You knew I was writing about you?"

"Of course I knew." he said as he took off his gloves and placed them on the counter.

"Where's your chariot?" I asked.

"Parked out back in the lot." he says pointing to my parking lot.

"You parked your chariot in the parking lot?
 No way."

I looked out my window to see his chariot parked in a parking space in the lot below.
 "Huh. It fits, perfectly like it was made for it. " I said

"It was made for it." he replied

 "No, parking lots are made for cars." I explained.

"Yes but cars got their size from the chariot." he answered.

 "You're talking crazy now. Cars came out way after chariots were long gone. I thought the Chariot card would have a little more sense between the ears." I replied.

 He looked at me and said "Let me explain. I know you are just a peasant author so I will try not to confuse your simple mind too much."

"I'm not a peasant." I said

"Ok …listen little peasant man. Sit down!." He said as if he wasn't listening to my response at all.

"The first long distance roads built in Europe were built by the Roman Empire. These well planned accomplishments were carefully thought out. The width of a road was to be able to accommodate two horses walking side by side when hitched to a chariot or wagon."

"OK, so what's that got to do with anything now?" I asked

"As time went on we expanded our roadways. We kept the same road width and never questioned it. It was just the width of a road. Because of this centuries old road width, cars were designed to be able to drive down those same roads." he continued.

"So the width of cars were decided on widths of existing roads. Even before cars, the railroad era kept this standard in place. Tracks were thought of as roads for the train to use."

"So today your roads and train tracks are built by the measure of a horse's ass just like they always were."

"No one ever questioned changing that width. They could have, but no one ever thought to. So naturally my chariot will fit into a parking space in your lot just like a glove."

"Nah….really?" I asked.

"Really…..little peasant man." he said with a smile.

"Im not a peasant man!" I said

"So how's this book coming Vincent?
Will other peasants read it?" he said.

"Not sure really. Still shaping it up at this point." I answered.

"Don't give it too much thought Vincent. You'll over think it."

"Well I got to be careful of how it goes don't I?" I said.

"How much thought do you give when having conversations with friends Vincent?" he said while looking out my window.

"It just flows I guess." I said

He turned to me and said "Exactly. This book is about conversations correct?"

"Yeah" I replied.

"When you get together with friends and talk you don't carefully plan out what to say before you meet them. It just flows. That's conversation. That's the trick Vincent. You feel comfortable talking with these cards just like old friends. So it should just move forward effortlessly."

"That's the whole objective of what it is you're trying to accomplish with this book." he continued. "Casual conversations with your old friends the 22 Major Arcana."

"If you understand what it is you're doing you will have the confidence to do it. You are an accomplished professional Tarot reader. Right Vincent?"

"Yes. That's true. For many years now." I said rather proudly."

"So, you see, your tiny little peasant mind flows with thought as you look at these cards. Then you gain confidence in your work."

"You know what you're doing with those cards. You understand the workings behind the application." he said. "You have that insight." That is to your advantage over others trying to do what it is you do. Read Tarot cards."

"Today that new information on the application of reading Tarot cards can be found and learned. The mystics who lead the way did not have that information. They argued and disagreed with each other over theories of the workings of the Tarot. Tiny peasant minds can't help it. Their theories were all inconsistant and vague."

"But thanks to you we have those conclusive facts on the Tarot today. You found them Vincent. That is the energy of the Chariot card working within you."

 "You disagreed with the Tarot masters of the past Vincent. You questioned what they taught. The big names like Papus, Crowley, Waite, Levi to name a few."

"The pages of your books show that although you're still a peasant."

"You could be criticized for your radical thinking on this centuries old subject. But that didn't stop you. That's a leadership quality.
 People are like sheep. They all do what everyone else is doing in the flock. You stood out from the rest of that flock."

"Hey I like that. Thanks." I replied.

"Well you're still a peasant sheep, a black sheep, that's all. But at least that made you stand out from all the other sheep."

"Im not a sheep." I said.

He agreed saying "True…your just a simple peasant man."

"Im not a peasant either!" I yelled back.
"I'm a professional Tarot reader!"

I went on saying "That mindset of the Tarot being unexplainable and mysterious is centuries strong and it is hard to get others to see what I see. What is so obvious to me seems wrong to many others in the craft."

He looked at me and said "That is your challenge. You are trying to lead the way to a different path with the Tarot and how it is understood. And that new understanding allows you to see more about what it is you are doing with these cards. A wider range of understanding gives you more confidence when things are challenging with your work."

"Wow. I never thought about it that way but I agree. Most readings are unique and have their own little snags here and there to fine tune and make clear." I said

"Yes. And because you know those primitive cards so well you are not worried about those little snags during your readings. Because you know how to fix them." He said. "You are a self proclaimed master of the Tarot. Do you know anyone else who calls themselves that Vincent?"

"No. Just me." I said.

"Although you're a peasant you can still be comfortable with that claim. You know what you can do with those cards without giving it too much effort. You teach the Tarot to many others. And what do you stress the most in your lessons."

"Confidence in what they see in the cards." I said.

"Yes. Confidence. I've seen you teach Vincent. You always make it a point to let the student know that what they see in those cards is just as "correct" as what you see in the cards. You teach them to be confident in themselves."

"That their ideas are wonderful and unique. Just like everyone else. Everyone has the ability to ride the Chariot with confidence once they understand how to use it." He said.

"Do you like to ride that chariot?" I asked.

"Yes." He said.

"Why?" I asked.

"The chariot in combination with the war bow was the first weapon of mass destruction. A group of ten charioteers with war bows could circle around an army of a 1000 men on foot armed with spears who would be defenseless against them. A thousand men on foot could travel at 3mph."

"The chariot gave man the opportunity, for the first time to travel up to 20mph, effortlessly. Those ten charioteers could circle around an army of a thousand men shooting arrows into them from 200 yards away who would not be able to fight back in any way."

"Wow. A history lesson from a Tarot card." I said.

"Now you know why the Chariot is in the Tarot. It was something that couldn't be beat. It was considered indestructible. Invincible in it's time. But only once you knew how to control one and how to shoot arrows with a war bow. Then you were confident in your quest of winning." He said.

"I would rather have a 1966 GTO." I said.

"That would be your chariot then?" he asked.

"Yeah. Black 1966 GTO ragtop with a 389, four-barrel, 3-speed on the floor and high performance shocks too! Oh and chrome wheels. 0 to 60 in 6.5 seconds flat. Now that's a chariot! Ha!"

"You wouldn't be able to handle it Vincent. Not to it's fullest potential that is. You are not a professional race car driver. You're just a simple peasant man."

"Yeah but I would have fun trying."

"That is not your chariot Vincent. Your chariot is a deck of Tarot cards. That is where you shine best. Not driving cars. Your confidence is with a deck of 78 mysterious cards that has been around for centuries. A deck of cards that can foresee the future. That is your chariot my friend." He said. "Not a 66 Pontiac GTO."

"I guess you're right. I never could drive a stick very well anyway."

"There are three basic rules to become great at something."

"What's the first rule?" I asked.

"The first rule to mastering something is to use what you are naturally good at. Your talent. Don't focus on trying to be good at something you're weak in. Fine-tune something you are good at and you can become GREAT at it instead of just good."

"Can I at least practice something I'm weak at?"

"Fine. Practice something you are weak at and you can become good at it. But if you practice something you are naturally good at, you can become amazing."

"So becoming a professional race car driver is out?" I asked.

"Don't even think about it Vincent."

"What's the second rule?" I asked.

"The second rule to being a master at anything is understanding you will never know it completely."

"Well I know everything about those cards don't I?" I asked.

"No. You just think you do Vincent. Typical peasant mentality." He said.

"OK genius, what's the third rule?" I asked.

"The third rule?"

"Yeah. What is it?" I asked

"The third rule is…You make the rules. Don't listen to what others say are the rules. Create your own rules. Don't focus on what others have done. Focus on what others say cannot be done. Then do it!"

"Cool!" I said.

"Anymore rules?" I asked.

"Sure, All sorts of them." He said.

"Wha-?" I asked.

"That's for you to find out." He said.

"What! Come on! Tell me."

"That's enough for now. See ya later." He said.

"Wait! Come on tell me more!"

"You've got a long way to go Vincent." He said.

"Well tell me more then. Come on!"

With that he walked out the door. "Damn! Wish he coulda told me more."

"He was really cool! I wish I would have wrote that information down."

"Oh well I still think having a black 1966 GTO would be really cool. Would rather think about that instead Tarot cards any day!"

He came back into my apartment and grabbed his gloves off my counter top and said "You're a Tarot card reader Vincent. Quit daydreaming about old muscle cars."

"But I do wanna 66 GTO!"

"Write your book!" With that he walked out again. I looked out my window to see the chariot was gone. In it's place was a black convertible 66 GTO and the charioteer was getting into it! As he opened the driver side door he looked up at my window and mouthed the word ….PEASANT to me with a smile.

He got into that GTO, turned over that 389 and that old goat growled as he slowly coasted out of my parking lot. I thought to my self… "Now that's a chariot! Oh well, I've gotta book to write."

Chapter 8   Strength

Fluffy?

Sitting at my computer thinking that I've got to get back on track with my writing.
 I've been sitting here doing nothing for a few days now. Nothing getting done.

Just wasting my time. As I take another swig of wine I hear loud purring coming from behind me. I turn to my right and see a huge lion sitting on my bed!

That's when a woman taps me on my left shoulder and says "You better get your act together."

 "Whoa! Who are you? That's a lion over there!"

"Ah come on Vincent. You're writing about the Tarot right? Remember STRENGTH?"

 "OK, Yeah ….the Strength card. Wow that's a big lion over there." As I watch that big cat just sitting there on my bed looking over at me.

"You need to wake up Vincent." She says as she takes my glass of wine away from me and pours it down the sink.

"Hey! That's my wine!"

"You don't need anymore of that today. It's not even noon yet." She says as she starts cleaning my work area.

"Hey that's my stuff!" I said as she takes my ashtray and pack of cigarettes off my desk.

"You are putting things off Vincent. You know you're just letting the days fly by with nothing to show for them. Sitting here thinking about what you are going to do is fine but you also need to act on those ideas too. You're becoming a statue here at this table. You need to change your daily pattern Vincent. That helps break old habits. You can start by cleaning this place up. Look at this place! Is that a bench-press over there?" She asked

"Yes. I work out sometimes." I said

"Ha! When have you used that thing last? It seems like you use it more as a place to throw your dirty clothes." She says as she looks at the pile of clothes covering up the bench-press.

"Well it's been a few days since I worked out."

"More like a few months." She says
 "It's starting to show too Vincent. Too much wine, cigarettes and junk food while sitting here on your butt."

"Hey that lion of yours is chewing on my pillow!" I said

Fluffy! Stop that!" She says to the giant feline laying on my bed. That big cat looks up at her for a moment and then continues chewing on my pillow.

"Fluffy?" I asked

"Yes that's her name." the woman said with a smile.

"Well Fluffy needs to get off my bed!"

"I think she's letting you know that you need to get back to work on your books and quit lying around here."

"Hey you! Quit chewing on my pillow!" I yell out at the lion.

She stops for a moment, looks at me, and then continues gnawing away, only this time she's purring as well.

Purrr…Purrr…Purrr

"Vincent it's easy to find excuses to put things off till another day but you need to stay strong on your goals. What have you done this week? Nothing!"

"I'm just taking a break. A vacation. Hey Fluffy is destroying my pillow!" I said

"Oh so sitting here drinking your wine is a vacation?" She says as she picks up an empty wine bottle from the floor and tosses it in my trash can.

"Look at this dusty book self. All these books on the Tarot. When have you looked at them lately?"

"I already read them." I answered.

"Sure you did. A number of times and you know all that information I'm sure, but didn't those books motivate you to write your own? Those wonderful authors, Sally Nichols, Stuart Kaplan, Papus, Mary K. Greer, Rachel Pollack, Eden Grey."

"You wanted to become like them. And here you sit. With all your knowledge going to waste. These authors motivated you once. Read them again and you will get that feeling right back Vincent."

"Yeah, maybe tomorrow I will look at them and dust that self off a little too." I said looking at the dusty self.

"Hey lady, Fluffy is chewing on my pillow again!" I said as we both looked at that big feline laying there on my bed with my pillow between both paws, chewing away.

"FLUFFY! Stop that!" She said.

The lion stopped, looked at us both and then continued chewing my pillow while purring.

Purrrr purrrrr purrrrr.

"Now my pillow is gonna have lion spit all over it!" I said.

"She likes your bed Vincent."

"Yeah well I like my bed too!"

" Doesn't look like it.
You haven't made that bed in weeks." she said.

"You need to shape up Vincent. What you got in this refrigerator?" She said as she looked inside. "Mmmm. A bottle of ketchup, a half loaf of bread, One, two, three….five bottles of wine! What's this? Looks like a bag of raisins."

"I think those were grapes once. I eat out most of the time." I said.

"What is this?" She said as she held a small clear bag out to me.

"I don't know what that is. Mystery food. Give it to Fluffy and see if she eats it." I answered with a laugh as I lit a cigarette. I looked over at Fluffy who was now laying on her side giving a big yawn looking at us both as she stretches out with my pillow between her front paws. .

Purrrr purrrrr purrrr.

"Vincent. Read these books on your shelf again. You need to get motivated. You need to find your true strength. It's too easy for you to put things off and do nothing. These books are what inspired you to write your own. You need a spark!"

"Can't seem to find it lately. "I said

"That's because you're not looking in the right places Vincent."

"Whaddya mean?"

"Who are you?" She asked

"You already know who I am. You been saying my name."

"That's just a word Vincent. A word your mother gave you when you were born. But who are you?" She asked again.

"In order to find your strength you have to know who you are. That is key. Know who you are and know what you are up against when you take on a challenge."

"A challenge?" I asked.

"Yes, like getting your act together and writing your next book. That's your challenge at this time."

"Most people don't know who they are. Not really anyway. Know who you are completely and you can accomplish many things." she said as she took a dusty book off my shelf.

"Wow. OK. How do I find out who I am then?" I asked.

"Take a deep look within and you will start to know yourself. But you have to look to begin with. That's where strength lies Vincent. In knowing who you really are. Not what people call you but who you are. You would still be the same person if you were named Sam instead of Vincent. The name doesn't change who you really are. You make the name. The name doesn't make you."

"I'll stick with Vince. I don't feel like a Sam. I feel more like a Vince…I think."

"The world is yours once you see your strength Vincent. People don't realize that about themselves. But it's true.
 Finish writing your book. You have a lot to offer on the Tarot. That's one of your strengths. You have many Vincent."

"I do?" I asked

"Yes, you do."

I looked over to see Fluffy laying on her back with my wet pillow between her front paws looking over at us both.

Purrr purrr purrr.

"Finish your book Vincent."

"Finish it? I feel stuck right now. Just drawing a blank. Not sure where to even start with it."

"Start at the end." she replied.

"What? The end? That doesn't make any sense." I said

"Sure it does Vincent. Visualize the end of your book. And then work backwards to the beginning."

"Wow! You wanna be my editor? You have some good ideas."

"I'm not here to edit your book. I'm here to point out your strong points. Find your center Vincent. Focus on your goals."

Meanwhile Fluffy is sitting there on my bed with her back to us – looking out my window at the birds."

"Can you get Fluffy off my bed please!" I asked

Fluffy looks back at us as if she knows her name. Then she rolls around on my bed looking at us again.

Purrrr purrrr purrrr.

"The problem I have with my work is getting people to see what I see in the Tarot cards.
 That's the hardest thing to get across. Sometimes I feel I fail at reaching some people."

"Well remember not to be afraid of failure Vincent. Failure also means learning and learning gives you strength. People who are afraid of failure would rather do nothing instead of failing. That is not living at all. That is just mimicking life and going through the motions."

"Wow sounds deep to me." I said as I took a drag off my smoke.

"Hey why don't you get a pet hamster instead of that huge lion?" I asked

Fluffy hisses at me and bites more on my pillow.

"We get along just fine Vincent." She answered.

With that she said "Come on Fluffy. Let's go girl."

Fluffy immediately jumps off my bed and went to her side as they both walk out the door. On her way out she said "Remember Vincent, know who you really are. It's just a matter of finding where you keep it hidden. Most people keep it hidden way down inside themselves. You're stronger than you realize Vincent. You just gotta reach for it and you'll see it's there for you."

After the door closed behind her I went to my fridge and grabbed another bottle of wine. Sat back down at my computer and crushed out my cigarette. I thought about what just happened….looking over at my chewed up pillow I thought……wow….Fluffy was pretty cool.

Chapter 9   The Hermit

We know there's a mole

Sitting here late at night wondering what I can write about the Hermit, number 9.
That card can stand for hidden knowledge. Answers that need to be found. I always liked this card. The Hermit just seems so isolated and wise with hidden wisdom.

That's when the phone rings. Who would be calling me this late at night!
I pick up my phone and say "Hello?"

A low voice on the other end says "We need to talk.....I'll be at your place in 5 minutes" *Click*.

"WHAT! Who's coming over here now! It's after midnight! Some kook?! It must be a wrong number." I went back to my computer and continued writing.

Soon I hear footsteps coming down the hall way. "Someone's coming home late?" I thought to myself.
The footsteps stop outside my door and I hear a soft *"knock....knock...knock"* on my door.

What?!! Who could that be?

I open my door and the Hermit is standing there in his long cowl robe. He walks in uninvited. As he looks around my room he sets his lantern down on my desk and closes my drapes. Then he says "Kill the lights"

"How about if I just turn them down? What's this all about?" I asked as I lowered the lights.

"You seem to be getting a lot of sensitive information about us Vincent.
Who's your connection?" he says as he grabs my phone and takes out the battery.

Hey that's my phone!

"Affirmative" he says...."It might be bugged."

We know there's a mole Vincent. Who are you working for?"

"A mole? Whattya mean a mole?" I asked

"A rat Vincent!" he answered

"A rat and a mole? Here? Any farm animals?" I answered
"Maybe a cow?"

"Don't be funny." he answered
"Where are you getting your information from? Who you workin for? The *Angel Cards* perhaps? We need to know now before it's too late." he said looking at me sternly.

"I don't know what you're talking about." I answered.

"I have all night Vincent.... Tell me, how do you explain these documents?" he says as he tosses both of my books on the table.

"Those are my books" I answered

"Ah! – So you admit it then!"

"Yeah, My name and picture are printed on the backs. See?? showing him the covers.

"Don't be coy Vincent. Who's the mole? Our sources think the Angel cards are behind this. – We can do this the easy way or we can do this the hard way" he says. Then he hits me in the shin with his staff a few times.

whack whack

"Hey! Cut that out!" Crazy guy comes in here, hitting me on the shin with a stick.

"We have quite a large file on you Vincent Pitiscki" he said as he pulls out a folder from his robe.

Uh...the name is PITISCI not PITISCKI" I said. Rubbing my shin bone.

"Oh, thanks. I'll make a note of that." and he erases the K on his paper.

"Vincent we can't allow you to continue with your work. You are destroying the very essence of what we are." he says as he peeks out of my drapes making sure he wasn't followed.

"Whattya mean destroying?" I asked
"I thought I was helping"

"For centuries we've been able to keep the Tarot's mysterious knack of accurate predictions a secret. Occultist names like *PAPUS, WAITE, CROWLEY, CASE, LEVI* and many more searched, yes! But we stopped them and we'll stop you too Vincent."

"Who are you? A common reader who just happens to stumble on our secret? We find that hard to believe Vincent. Who is your connection. Who's your contact. Is it the *Ten of Wands*? He's been acting strange lately."

"You are trying to expose our deepest secret. And that mystery is what makes the Tarot so curious to people. It's mysterious and unexplainable ability to predict the future Vincent! Which is the only reason people are intrigued by us. If your work leaks out, it will destroy us. We can't let that happen Vincent. We can't allow you to reveal that centuries old mystery!"

"Whattya gonna do? Hit me with your stick again?" Ha!

He whacks my shin again....*whack whack*

"Hey! Cut that out!" I said as I grab the stick from his hand. "Hey...this thing is just hollow molded plastic. What you gonna do?... Annoy me to death with a plastic stick!" Ha!

"Well I'll admit we're not very good at 'strong arm' tactics. We never had to go this far before. I was hoping playing *Good Card – Bad Card* would get you to cooperate." he said

"But there is only one of you here" I said.

"I was multi-tasking." he said

"Look don't worry. I'm not out to destroy the Tarot. But if people can understand why it works can you imagine the improvements that could be made in doing readings with you guys?" I said

"No, I can't Vincent. Are there any?" He replied with a curious look.

"Yes! Lots of improvements can be made once the application is seen for what it is. Explaining why it works opens up new doors of understanding.
Trust me the Tarot will be better off for it. There's no mole telling me your secrets. Today we know more than we did when the Tarot first came around. It's a great method to find answers and it works. Now it can be shown why it works with clear conclusive facts based on psychological research and study. It's a new age my friend." I explained

"So the Tarot will benefit from taken the mystery out of it?" he said

"Of course it will. Because it opens up newer doors of mystery. The mystery of the mind and using it's wonderful capabilities." I replied

"Better than before? No more scepticism! No more bad mouthing what we are as a silly fantasy. We would be a legitimate source of ideas?" he said, looking at me with surprise.

"Yeah – That's right!!" I said

"Well, wait till the others hear about this! We'll have a celebration for sure! You're taking us out of the darkness Vincent!
Is your shin OK? Sorry about that." he said with concern.

"Yes, it's fine I said as I rubbed my leg. Molded plastic staff huh? Like a *whiffle* staff? Ha! Well, it looks very realistic." I said handing it back to him.

"Look it – You know I love all you guys. I've had you around for many years. Actually I don't know what I would do without you."

"Really Vincent?"

"Really Hermit." I said

"So there's no mole? And this getting leaked out to the public won't destroy interest in the Tarot?" he asked.

"Nah! It will make it even better. We know more about the mind and how to use it today. Imagine the possibilities this could bring if people really understood why the Tarot works. They would be able to improve on it. Make it more proficient. And learn to read in ways never done before. Better ways. That's why I write books about the Tarot.

If you understand how something works you can improve on it. You guys will be better than ever. All 78 of you. Trust me."

"Vince, you're the best. I wish you were one of us. A new Tarot card added to the family. The Vince card!"

Ha! " If you added me into the Tarot – what would I represent?" I asked

I dunno. We'd figure something out for you. Maybe 'Vince-ness.' *A time to focus on 'vince-ness'* he replied thinking out loud.

"Wha? What's vince-ness?" – I asked.

"I dunno. We would work out those details later on" he said

"Well thanks but I like the relationship as it stands right now. No need to change it. Besides, I don't think anyone is trying to attain *'vince-ness'* in their lives"

"Ah, maybe you're right. So we're cool Vince?" he asked

"Yes, we're fine Hermit."

With that he smiled, shook my hand, said goodbye and walked out.

As he closed the door behind him I sat thinking about what's just happened. Then I noticed the lantern still sitting on my desk. Oh well, I guess he'll be back. Nice lantern.

Hey! I wonder if this thing's bugged!

Chapter 10 The Wheel
Do you know the time?

As I looked at the Tarot card *The Wheel of Fortune* I thought what a curious card. One creature is rising up one side of the wheel and another creature is descending downward on the wheel with a sphinx sitting at the top as if not moving at all.

I guess we all have our ups and downs. This card seems to show me that in time all things must pass. But what is time? The wheel in that card reminds me of a clock face measuring time itself. I seem to understand the concept of time but yet if I had to explain what time is to someone else … I wouldn't be able to do it.

I wonder if time really exists. Or is it just a man made perception.

Then I hear a voice say " Excuse me…. Do you know the time?"

I turn around and see a life size image of that card right in my room! WOW!! And the sphinx sitting on top looking at me with a grin.

"Holy Cow! What did you ask me?"

"I said…Do you know the time?" The sphinx replied.

I look at my watch and say "Yes. It's 10:05."

The sphinx looks at me and says "Wrong answer!"

"No that's right" as I give my watch a second look.

That sphinx looked at me and said "Did you understand my question?"

"Of course I understood your question. You asked me what time it was and I told you it's 10:05! Geez .... crazy sphinx."

The sphinx looked at me with a grin and said again. "That was not an accurate answer to a simple question."

"You don't know what you're talking about." I replied

Then the sphinx said "I didn't ask you to tell me the time. I just asked if you knew the time. If you knew the correct time then your answer should have simply been …..*Yes*."

"Oh I see. You're a sphinx so you ask tricky questions. Why would you be so concerned to know if I knew the time? Whaddya care if I know the time?"

"I was just curious seeing time doesn't really exist at all. You just have that little machine on your wrist telling you a number. You assign a man made perception to that and call it "*the time*". A label, an insignificant notch." said the sphinx.

"OK, well then you tell me what time it is if you're so brilliant. Go ahead, tell me." I said pointing at the sphinx.

"I don't give silly things like time a second thought." the sphinx said as if brushing my question aside with his hand.

"Do you really believe in this thing you call time?" he asked

"Well sure I do. I have to." I said pointing to my clock on the wall.

"Oh how nice another machine mounted on your wall. tick toc tick toc. Very impressive Vincent."

"What is time then?" he asked

"Not too sure. But I know it exists." I said

"What says it exists Vincent? That machine on your wall? Tick tock tick tock." he asked laughing.

"Well I don't know. It's just there." I replied

"Yeah it's there because you made it up! Can time stop?" he asked.

"I don't know. You tell me. You seem to know all about it." I said

"Well you can't stop something that doesn't exist in the first place. This time thing that you believe so strongly about moves along a horizontal path from left to right like yesterday…then today…then tomorrow right?" he asked.

"Well of course….yeah.". I replied.

"Time is cyclic not linear. What year is it?" he asked

"2022" I replied.

"Oh yeah 2022 AD right?"

"Yeah right!" I nodded.

"So two thousand and twenty three years ago we were in BC right?" he asked.

"Of course…yeah!" I said.

"Ha!!!! That is soo lame! Ha!!" So did people living… Let's say in the year 50BC, did they know that the next year was going to be 49BC? Did they say to each other 'well see ya next year when it's gonna be 49BC."

"Wow don't the years just fly by. Seems like only yesterday it was 53BC! Ha!! Remember back in the good ol days way back in 75BC? Wow they must have really had a big New Years Eve party in 1BC. That night would be the start of AD! The year 0! Ha ha!!
It's all nonsense. You number the cycles and call them dates in time. Hilarious!"

"Numbers have nothing to do with time. That is only in your mind. It's the same year as last year and the year before that. Time moves like this wheel. It spins in cycles but stays in place. It doesn't travel forward down some path."

"You carefully record all events with time. Dates this or that happened. So what. Your own birth is recorded in time. So what. If anything is recalled throughout the cycles of this planet .... people will always start out by saying "When did that happen? When was it? As if that is a factor to know a date on a calendar. People say *My birthday is coming, I'm gonna have fun that day.*" Why wait! Have fun every day!"

"Anniversaries people spend time appreciating their partners that day. A day of love. Make everyday a day of love for that person! Why wait for a once a year time to do that!"

"Where are you on the wheel of time?" said the sphinx

"I dunno. In some ways I'm going up and in others ways I'm going down so it's hard for me to say." I've been reading the Tarot cards for 50 years in 2019 so in that respect I feel that is an accomplishment. Going up." I answered.

"You can't understand it all until you know where you sit in time itself." he said

"Where am I sitting on that wheel then?" I asked

"Look and see. Look closely." he said

As I gazed into the spinning wheel.... Images started to appear. I can see myself a long time ago. "Hey! Is that me?" I said as I see a young teenage boy with shoulder length hair sitting at the kitchen table reading Tarot cards. The family is sitting all around me as I read the cards for them.

" Next I see me at a psychic fair getting my cards read. The reader says she sees me working with Tarot cards and if I become an artist to sign my work on the left hand side of my paintings. Next I see me putting my Tarot cards under my pillow before I go to sleep. I remember doing that too! "

"Here I am in Old Town going to all the head shops getting black light posters of Escher drawings for my room. Sitting in my room reading the "*Seed Underground Newspaper*" wearing black knee high suede boots! Wow, I walked around in public like that?!"

"Is that Lynda! I see her and me sitting together talking about reading on the psychic scene. Wow! She was beautiful! Here's our wedding day. I see us in our house too. Both still reading strong. What a ride that has been. Thirty years together as pro readers and still going strong."

"That's where you're wrong." he said.

"It is one experience and has nothing to do with your calendar. It is just many cycles not years. Cycles is all. Only one time….many cycles."

"No – that was 1993 when we met." I replied.

"No you just put a number on that spinning wheel and call it a date in time. But you haven't moved. The experience has moved around you that's all.

You measure time. Numbering time is just a mode of thought. The universe never started and it will never end. So how can you measure it's age? You make the idea up in your mind of time passing by. It spins by you in a circle. It doesn't pass you by in a line."

"Besides, you don't even do a very good job of measuring this thing you call time. How many minutes in a day Vincent?"

"Hell I don't know." I said.

"You seem to take time soooo seriously you think you would know a simple thing like that but you don't. You're a 70 year old man and have seen many minutes go by in your life. You think you would know by now how many minutes there are in one small day." said the sphinx as he laughed.

"Well you tell me if you're so smart. How many?" I asked

"1440 minutes in a day Vincent. Ten thousand eighty minutes in a week. Five hundred twenty four thousand and one hundred sixty minutes in a year. On your 70th birthday you had experienced a total of thirty six million, six hundred ninety one thousand and two hundred minutes. There, now you can keep track of that too. Tic tock tic tock. Ha!!" laughed the sphinx.

"Hey I gotta question for you. How it is you stay in place at the top of that spinning wheel so cool and calm?"

"That's just an illusion Vincent. Like time is an illusion." replied the sphinx.

"But you're sitting on top of a spinning wheel." I said.

"There is no top to a wheel Vincent." he answered.

"Yea. I'm looking right at ya doin it."

"Who says I'm sitting at the top Vincent?
A wheel's a circle right?". he said.

"Yeah, so what?" I replied.

"A circle doesn't have a top to it Vincent. Or a bottom or a left side or right side does it?" explained the sphinx.

"You're really sitting in the center of your own circle Vincent. You're not moving at all. Events in the physical realm are moving around you, which includes your physical body by the way."

"My body?" I asked.

"You are not that body. The body is something you witness just like the rest of this world you're in. You're perception of your very existence is centered around a spinning universe that you are witness to. That creates the illusion of things passing you by going "down the road" becoming the past and heading towards the future." he replied.

Looking at my clock the sphinx said "Hey Vincent you've got to get going. Look at the time! 11:05!"

"OMG yes I'm running late. I start today at noon!"

"Well you better get going Vincent or you will be walking into work imagining you are late again."

"Oh that's all right. I'll just tell everybody that I'm not late. That's just their imagination. I can never be late because time doesn't exist. There .... that's easy."

"Better run along now Vincent. That little machine on your wrist is ticking away the minutes of time! Just remember…you're not really going anywhere. You're just spinning in place. Have fun spinning around and counting the minutes of your day Vincent.
Tic tock tic tock."

I better call work..........*ring ring ring ring*
"Hello?"

"Yeah Joey? It's Vince. I'm running a little late. I'm walking out the door now."

"AGAIN??!!"

Chapter 11 Justice

Words

As I sat at my desk looking over the things I wanted to cover in my book, I heard someone clear their throat. But there's no one here but me. Then I heard a loud banging like metal on stone! It echoed through my small apartment! Wow! Someone has a broken water pipe? That's when a set of scales was thrown in front of me! *Crash!* I looked down at the scales, and they were right next to the Justice card. And there she was, the lady of Justice leaning over in her throne, looking right at me.

"Court's in session!" she blared out.

I looked twice and blinked my eyes, but she didn't go away. "Hello," I said, acknowledging her presence.

"Well, here you are, putting words into your book."

"Yes, that's true," I said. "Words come in handy when writing a book, wouldn't you agree?"

"Well, words have their place, yes," she answered back as she casually picked off some lint from her gown. "But they are overrated, you know," she said, sitting with those deep eyes staring right through me.

"How so?" I asked.

Then she leaned forward and said, "Did you know that ninety-three percent of what we communicate to others is nonverbal? That is to say, only seven percent of how we communicate with others is through words. Still think words mean a lot? Your intent is going into that book more than the words are.

"The real justice system can't be debated or denied. True justice is based on universal principles—not on words. Your US Constitution and your Declaration of Independence represent truth. But how those words are perceived depends on the individual.

"You have nine Supreme Court Justices who read the same words called your US Constitution who cannot unanimously agree on what those words say. Real justice is truth and has no book of laws to interpret. It just is, and that's that. Authority isn't always truth.

Truth is authority.

"In your country you have the right to life, liberty, and the pursuit of happiness. That's cute. You also have the right to death. For without death, you have no life. Justice is based on duality in your world: Good and evil. Right and wrong. Mankind puts one against the other and tries to interpret which is which. Muslim, Jew. Black, white. Gay, straight. Republican, Democrat. No one focuses on truth. They're too busy hating and fearing the other side. Going through life with blinders on."

"Wow," I said, striking a match to light a cigarette and wondering where this was all going.

Justice looked at me with a smile and continued. "If the whole world was only good, and there wasn't any evil, you would never know what good is. It would just be the norm. The same holds true with love. If you loved everyone, you would never know that love ever existed. In your world, you cannot understand or perceive anything if it has no duality to it. This is why God is such a puzzle to mankind. God has no duality.

"Know this, Vincent: nothing exist except God. There is no 'outside' of God. God has no edges to it. God is in everything. Which means it's OK to feel you are a part of God. But the physical plain is all dualities: Space and matter. Time, life, death, love, fear, happiness, and sorrow. What you really are is a part of this universe you call God. You are immeasurably old and have taken on millions of different shapes and forms and the coming and going of those shapes and forms are just a universal pulse of an eternal *one*: God.

"You are the universe witnessing and experiencing itself from billions of different points of view. Each one of you is a point of view. And the coming and going of these points of view keeps things moving along—evolving and changing all the time for a different look. This way the feeling of what you really are is constantly changing. That keeps things interesting, doesn't it?"

"Wow. Sounds kinda scary, actually," I said.

"Oh? So change scares you? Why? Because it is the unknown. That's why. Don't be such a candy-ass," she shot back, pointing that big sword toward me.

"Hey! Don't get so touchy. I'm just trying to understand!" I snapped. "You're talking words, universe, and god and all this stuff; I'm just trying to write a book."

"Ah, don't take it so personal," she replied. "It's supposed to be a little scary. If it wasn't challenging, it would be kinda boring around here, wouldn't it? So it's sorta like a roller coaster ride for approximately seventy or eighty years," she explained as she waved her sword tip up and down.

"That's a long time!" I said.

"Is it?" she replied. "You have nothing but time. You are eternal. You're part of the most perfect thing there is. You are a part of the universe. You have nothing to gain. What can you possibly gain when you already are *everything* to begin with," she said as she looked into my eyes. The real law of justice is this: When you enter this physical plane, you forget who and what you really are. Which is eternal perfection. Otherwise, being here while knowing you were eternal would just be soooo boring."

"I'm trying to evolve myself. Become enlightened. Be better than what I am all the time, but sometimes it's not easy," I replied.

"Enlightenment? You come down here into this physical arena limited to just five senses for a short time because it is challenging. It is enriching. So live the physical plane. Experience it," she said.

"Why is it necessary if I'm perfect already?" I said.

"It's not necessary," she replied. "It's enriching. Dancing isn't necessary, but the soul likes it. Painting a picture or being inspired in some way isn't necessary, but these things feed the soul.

They are like addictions! And that is what you do here. It's good for you to experience the physical."

"Addictions! I have the Justice card telling me addictions are good!" I said.

"You're born with addictions," she responded. "You are addicted to breathing, sleeping, eating, water, sex. Don't those things feel exhilarating when you want them and you get them? You are here to experience the physical plane. Which means you cannot survive without addictions."

Then she continued to say, "I get a real kick out of people who think they are supposed to deprive themselves of addiction to become more enlightened. Fasting on a mountaintop somewhere like a lump on a log.

That's exactly what they came from! Perfection. And that's exactly what they will be going back to. Perfection. So why come here to be exactly what you are to begin with? The reason you come here is to experience the physical. Not ignore it. To experience imperfection and challenge.

"Your religions that use the Bible as law have been contorted and twisted with words of confusion and contradiction. The Old Testament is based on "laws and judgment", but the New Testament is based on "love and grace". An eye for an eye, or turn the other cheek. Words. Take a closer look at your Bible. You will find all sorts of real life in it. Jesus wasn't religious; Jesus never said, 'The Kingdom of God is like a church service that goes on and on forever and never ends.' He said the kingdom was like a homecoming celebration, a wedding, a party, a feast to which all are invited. Like that song *'Cabaret': 'Come taste the wine, come hear the band, come blow your horn, start celebrating, right this way your table's waiting!'* Gosh! I love Liza! But seriously, enjoy your time here. Don't focus on what you feel are your faults. You are experiencing being mortal.

And that is a real change from what you really are. Immortal. Immortal and perfect."

I just stared like a deer caught in the headlights as she continued.

"As long as you live and let live, you are doing just fine being mortal. Love who you are, and accept your weaknesses, but have fun wrestling with them too. And remember, you are perfection. That is truth." With that, she picked up her scales from my floor and froze back into the card.

"Hey!" I called out. "You got sand all over my carpet!"

"So sue me," she replied as she faded off.

Chapter 12 The Hanged Man
Conformity

Planning on having guest over for dinner tonight. I'm very excited about it all. As I plan the evening I hear a voice from behind saying "So what you gonna have?"

I turn and see the Hanged Man sitting in one of my dining room chairs. "Well hello." I said

"Hi Vincent. Thought I might come by and help out. Mind if I....hang around?" He said with a grin.

"Thanks but I got it all figured out."

"I see we think the same." he said looking round my place

"Whattya mean?" I said

"Well reversal of ideas. That's what I stand for. Right? Reversal. And most people don't like that concept. It's uncomfortable to them. Hence the Hanged Man seems wrong doesn't it?"

"True" I answered "Kinda topsy turvy."

"People get freaked out if things aren't like they're used to. Your guest might not like this Vincent. Look at your dinner table. A 6' folding table that you normally keep folded up against the wall. Isn't that different? Most people have some expensive dining room table that stays in place all year long. In a room that is never used for anything else but dining on a few holidays each year.

"And how about these fancy chairs of yours? OOHH patio furniture chairs. Nice idea Vincent!" he says as he looks at the chair he's seated in.

"Yes it amazes me that more people don't use these. They only use these type of chairs to sit outside. Never inside the house. oohh no!!! That would be so wrong to do!" I answered.

"But they make so much more sense than big clunky wooden chairs. A nice set of six light weight patio chairs makes so much more sense to me. And you can stack them together and put them out of the way when your not using them." I said, putting the rest of the chairs in place.

"You and I think the same Vincent. That's why people see us as different than the rest of the world. We don't really fit in to the norm. Isn't that frustrating sometimes?" he asked.

"Sure it is, but that's their business, not mine" I said as I placed the dishes on the table for six."

"Are those dog dishes Vincent?"

"Why yes." I answered rather proudly. Showing him one of the chrome bowls. "I got'em at PETCO. Nice light weight chrome colored dog dishes. They don't tip and they don't break either. Great dishes. Dogs have better culinary than humans do.
Nothin like a good dog dish and a wooden spoon to eat beef stew with."

"Is that the main course tonight Vincent? Beef stew?"

"Yes, my superb beef stew recipe. Been in the crock pot since 5am this morning. Dinner served at 5pm this afternoon. Beef stew with my homemade corn bread."

"Some of your guest might be offended when they see you expect them to eat out of a dog dish Vincent."

"Well they were never used by a dog. I bought them brand new specifically for me."

"Might not make a difference Vincent. Remember you and I don't think like most others. New ideas aren't usually taken very well. Have your guest been here before?"

"No, This is a first time." I said.
"And these dishes work better than human dishes do. Dogs must be laughing at us when they see us eat out of those stupid, heavy, clumsy, breakable, ceramic bowls people use. They tip so easily!"

"There, the table is set nicely." I say as I look at the six placed chrome dog dishes laid out on the folding table with a nice wooden spoon at each one. And six white patio furniture chairs in place. "PERFECT! – I hope everyone comes hungry. We're gonna have a nice dinner and then we're gonna watch the game on TV. Starts at 6pm!"

"Serving any dessert?"

"Yes. Ice cream will be served as we watch the game."

"Where's the bowls for the ice cream?" he asked

"Oh yes. Almost forgot.
Here they are." I said as I place a plastic coffee mug at each setting.

"Coffee mugs! For ice cream!!??? Great idea Vince!"

"I agree! Better than a bowl. Insulated plastic coffee mugs keep the ice cream cold and you gotta handle on them to hold the ice cream in instead of balancing a bowl in one hand while trying to eat the ice cream with the other. Coffee mugs works better."

"Where's the TV?"

"In the other room." I said

He looks in the other room and sees the TV but no where to sit. "Where they gonna sit?" he asked.

"They can bring their patio chair with them into the TV room and sit where ever they like. Those chairs hardly weigh anything."

"Vincent, try to remember that most people don't see things the way you do, whether it makes sense or not, it is the way it is. Sometimes your perception of things might seem upside down but in reality might really make more sense."

"Like you, the Hanged Man, number 12 right?" I asked
"Hey, what should I call you anyway? I mean besides 'The Hanged Man."

"You can call me Darwin, DaVinci, Galileo, Tesla, Edison, Ford"

"OK – OK. I get it.
You said we're a lot alike.
So are you implying I have something in common with great minds like that?" I asked.

"Ha!" He laughed. "Only in a very small way my friend. But yes the same patterns are there. It's not that uncommon really. What you have going for you is you don't care that you're different. You don't try to be what you're not. You are you and that's that. And that's a good thing my friend."

"So the Hanged Man card can mean just thinking differently than others?" I asked.

"Sure it can Vincent. It can mean seeing things from a different perspective than the norm. And sometimes that is what is needed for great things to happen. Sometimes you may face ridicule for being different. But if the alternative means not being yourself, then isn't a little ridicule worth it. So sing when standing in line at the check-out counter. Dance down the street if you like. People will like to see someone just being themselves and not caring what others think of them."

Then I hear "DING-DONG."

"Oh! It's Five 0'Clock and my guests are here!!"

I open the front door and greet them all standing there together.

"Hiiiii!!!! Come on in!" Hugs and handshakes are exchanged. "Have a seat in the dining room. Make yourselves comfortable. I'll be right in there. Hope you like beef stew." I said as I walked into the kitchen to get the crock pot.

Chapter 13 Death

The Unknown

Sitting at my computer, working on the last chapter of my book, I glanced at my deck of tarot cards. The Death card appeared to be looking right at me.

I needed to take a break. Midnight already! As I rise and turn from my chair, I walk right into card number thirteen standing tall and still. Death!

"Uh! Aren't you a little early!" I said in a total shock.

"That's what most people say when I drop by," he answered.

Hoping to get on his good side, I said, "Uh, well, hello, Mr. Death card, uh. How are you? Uh, you look real good for yourself. Been working out? I wasn't expecting to see you so soon. Uh, I'm gonna be sixty, or I was."

"Ah. Don't get all excited; I'm not here for that. It's not your time yet."

"*Whew!* Thank God." I gasped, resting my forehead in both hands.

"Just heard you were writing about a few of the cards, so I thought I would drop by. I mean, I'm a pretty big name in the tarot, wouldn't you agree?" He said as he scraped a bony finger over the edge of that sickle.

"Yeah, big, but not too welcome," I replied.

"That's what I mean. I wanted to get that straightened out. I think I'm being misrepresented. I mean, come on now. It's not all that dramatic."

What: *dying?*" I shouted.

"Yes. Dying. You all must die at some time. So what's the problem? Why don't you just accept that simple and inevitable fact? It's a transition, that's all."

"A transition to what?" I asked.

"I could tell you – but then I'd have to kill you." he answered.

"Oh, now Death is a comedian," I said, rolling my eyes.

"But really, telling you would take all the fun out of living. People get too bent out of shape over dying. But the more you accept death as a reality of life, the more you live your life while here. It's a natural process. People that know I'm coming soon will tell you that.

They live each day and hour with eyes wide open, loving every minute. They become more alive. They realize how beautiful this wonderful gift of life is. Everyone else is busy thinking about trivial nonsense. People don't realize the impact they could have while here. Life is a play, and each of you are the leading role. Your performance can be good, or it can be lousy. Either way, at the end, you are going to say, 'So, how did I do?' Will others applaud your performance when it's over, or will they just walk away thinking it was no big deal? This is your time to shine. Put your heart into your life. Savor every minute. And make a difference. Leave with a standing ovation!"

"Wow, that was really a good sales pitch," I said. "But it still doesn't make you a welcomed sight. Sorry, but nooo thanks."

"Still afraid of dying? Why?"

"Because I don't know what happens afterward. That's why."

"It's not for me to tell you what happens after you leave here, but ask yourself this: What's the worst that could happen? *Nothing*. That's the worst that could happen. Nothing. You just go to sleep and never wake up again. Just nothing," he snapped back. "But if there is something more afterward, you're in like Flynn. Correct?"

I just stared with a blank expression at the skeletal figure before me.

"You still don't get it, do you?" he asked.

"I can't die yet. I'm writing a book," I said.

"Ah, don't worry about that. I'm not going to be back until after your book is finished."

"OK, then I'll take my time to finish it. Maybe another forty years!"

"So you want to live to be a hundred, then?"

"I don't know," I said. "I guess, yeah."

"Really? Have you ever visited a nursing home Vince? See those lucky one-hundred-year-old souls. Tell me if you feel they're happy. Their bodies still work, but it becomes difficult for the spirit to stay strong."

"I tell you what, Death. You're a real depressing pain in the ass, you know that? I was having a real good day until your bony ass came by."

"See ya soon, Vince."

"Yeah, that's what I'm afraid of. So take your time. Put me at the bottom of your to-do list, OK?"

"Finish your book, Vince."

"It's gonna take a looooong time to finish. It's a twenty-eight-volume encyclopedia set on dental floss."

"I know it's a book on the tarot, Vince."

"Hey, Death, I gotta skeleton joke for you: a skeleton walks into a bar and orders a beer …. and a mop. Get it?

Clock's ticking, Vince."

"OK, OK. Hey, really. I'm not going to be wearing no marble hat anytime soon, am I?"

"Tick tock, tick tock."

"Ya know what? You should get some Neosporin. Might help clear up that bony skeletal condition and improve your appearance."

"Vince, someday you will look just like me. And quit smoking those cigarettes. I don't plan on being back here for a while, and I'd hate to make a special trip."

With that, he froze back into the card.

Chapter 14   Temperance

Inspiration?

```
I've always had a difficult time understanding
the Temperance card-number 14.
```

"What to write here....What does that card mean –really. The image on that card is not really saying anything. She's just standing there pouring water from one urn to another. I always tell people that the Temperance card represents inspiration. Angels are here to inspire us. They have the power to help guide us on finding our passion."

Then I hear a voice say "I like that Vincent –That's good!
So have I inspired you then?"

I turn around in my chair and the Temperance angel is standing right behind me.

"WOW! Temperance! Hi!"

"Thought I would help out.
You're just staring at that screen so I felt you could use a spark."

"Well thanks."

"So you want that book you're writing to be successful don't you?"

"Yeah, I guess, yeah I do."

"Well you got a long way to go Vincent."

"But I think the book is coming along. Isn't it?" I said

"It's OK, but I think you can use a little boost.
Let's try this Vincent. Who in your life inspired you? Anybody?"

"I dunno. Lotta people did, I guess."

"Who? Think of someone specific who inspired you."

"I know. The Lone Ranger! He inspired me."

"OK. That's good Vincent. Now think of yourself as the Lone Ranger only with Tarot cards. That might help."

"I can do that, yes.
Actually I think I would make a real good Lone Ranger.
I can see that yes! Wearing a mask!
With my faithful Indian companion Toto!
Yes! Get a gun too! With silver bullets! I can see me now riding into the sunset on a white horse! Yeah!"

"The Indian companion was Tonto, Vince.
You're getting carried away. I just meant who inspired you. That's all. Like an example to motivate you forward."

"But I bet I would make a real good Lone Ranger!" I said

"Vincent...The Lone Ranger went out and captured dangerous criminals. You read Tarot cards. OK?"

"No, I really could do that though."

"Don't even think about it Vincent.
I don't need to see a 64 year old man walking down the street with a mask carrying a pistol. Your Lone Ranger career would only last a few blocks before the police threw you into the back of a squad car. OK? Just settle down."

"What? I could be the Lone Ranger if I wanted to!"

"No Vincent. You would probably hurt yourself so don't even think about it. Besides, you probably wouldn't know the difference between a horse and a giraffe. Let alone ride one. But you do have passion Vincent. And you have heart too. That much I'll give you. But you need to follow that passion Vincent. That's all I'm saying."

"I do." I said "I'm pretty good at my work aren't I?"

"You need more than just being good at something to be successful." she continued. "That's only a small part of success."

"It is? Well what am I missing then." I asked.

"You need to develop a strong interactive relationship with your following."

"What following? How do I do that?" I said

"You've stumbled upon something that is remarkable. In other words, something worth remarking about. You have found a way to explain in a logical and rational way why the centuries old Tarot has been such an amazing method to predict the future.

And when people see that, it will attract those who are listening. Create an interest that others of your profession can become a part of. Being sincere about it helps tremendously too. And you are sincere, I'll give you that." She said as she patted me on the shoulder.

"Figure out what people really want with the Tarot and give it to them. You know enough about the Tarot to do that Vincent."

"OK, well I'm already doing those things, aren't I? I'm sincere and I teach and write about it, right? How come it's still not hitting home then?" I asked

"You're not getting across to them. You're still blending in with the rest of the Tarot world. Everyone wants to blend in. Everyone wants to be right in the middle of it all and not stand out from the crowd. Everyone wants to be more average than average.

 That's not too inspiring Vincent. Look at the kids today. Getting a college degree with high grades. That's their goal. So now we have everyone with a college degree and high grades and just blending right in with all the others who have college degrees and high grades. You become average. You become the norm. It's so sad to see everyone wanting to be a perfect cog in the wheel of life."

"So being sincere and having something remarkable gets you out of that rut then?" I asked

"Well, no. There's more." she continued

"OK...what?" I asked as I drank my coffee.

"Stand out from the crowd. You're an artist. You're a genius. You all are genius. You just talk yourselves out of being that way. If what you create is unique and remarkable you will go far. You're just not taught how to do that. But if you follow what inspires you it will come naturally to you."

"Is that what you represent then? Inspiration?" I said

"I represent that flame in everyone. That passion that comes from the spirit within you. That is unshakable once you find it Vincent."

"But you're usually just seen as an angel pouring water from one urn to another. Many get confused with your real meaning."

"We give you inspiration Vincent. That is our gift to you. That is what living your life is all about. Finding what moves your soul. That is what we're here to guide you to find. Your passion. That's what keeps you alive. And I guide you on that path. Your guardian angel."

"What?! You're my guardian angel?!"

"Well of course I am. I am here aren't I?"

"Well where the hell have you been all this time?!"

"I'm 64 years old. About time you got here! My luck, I get a slacker guardian angel!"

"You haven't made my job easy Vincent. Actually I will probably get promoted after taking on this job."

"Manage your passion well; whether you teach the cards, read the cards, or write about them. Manage it well. Have others walk away from you with something valuable gained from the experience."

"And lead. Leading your following is important too.
Help them find what they seek."

"That's up to them isn't it?" I said.

"Not if you are a leader it isn't.
Show them how to do what they seek to do most.
You take that initiative. That's a leader. Set them on their path. Show them their options. That creates a following. Taking action. The knights in the Tarot deck stand for action. Be a knight. Take them somewhere on their quest. Lead them."

"But you need to inspire them too." she continued. "Inspiration can come from anywhere in the mix of things. It doesn't have to come from me up here at the top. It can come from regular people like yourself.

 Keep them interested and enthused about where they're heading and what they're doing. Show them their strengths and bring out their unique talents. Show them that being different has more value than blending in with the others. Show them that breaking away from the norm won't be the end of their world. It's the beginning!"

She poured more coffee into my cup from her urn and said "Good grades and a college degree are wonderful accomplishments to be proud of. But remember that all of you have unique qualities that sets you apart from the rest. And that is where your real value lies. Your individuality. What makes you –you? Your passion does that."

"Follow your passion Vincent. Act on things that move you. Finding a place where your uniqueness is sought and your passion is wanted. That is your quest in life. A knight search's for a quest." she said as she tossed the Knight of Cups from my deck down in front of me.

"You need to have a deep knowledge about your field in order to do that though. You already have that Vincent. You know those cards well enough. You are a Tarot geek Vincent! Hell you even know why they work. That makes you a leader right there. No one else sees that, do they?
But you do. "

I just sat their listening trying to absorb it all as I drank my coffee.

"You know more about the Tarot than most and you also broke open the biggest mystery of the Tarot. Why they work! With that breakthrough using the Tarot can now be a hundred times more effective than ever before. Now it can be improved, renovated, advanced. Because now people can understand why they work. It's no longer a mystery thanks to you. And you my friend, are the only one who ever saw it. You saw it because it was your true passion. So lead the way."

"Well thanks for seeing my talent. Coming from you that means something." I said

"What you are really doing is following your passion. That's the key. Not talent. Passion. Talent doesn't go very far without passion behind it. Passion is what makes you stand up and make it happen. Are you ready to act? If not, you don't have the passion. And the time to act is always right now. It's always been right in front of you. Just reach for it Vincent."

"I take some action here and there. I know what I'm doing. I'll be fine."

"No you don't. I see you and you're a slacker. You play things by ear all the time. You don't prepare anything. Not even your talks. You just go out there and start blabbing. Look at me – I'm talking. *Blab – Blab – Blab*. That doesn't work Vincent. You need to grab their interest. You can do that Vincent."

"Just grab it...it's right there in front of you. It would be so easy. Quit teasing yourself. Just reach a little bit further. It's that simple. My job is to just get you to see that. Then when you do, I'll be gone. Just...Like...That. POOF!"

When I blinked, the room was empty. Wow. I guess I was just day dreaming again. Better get back to my book. Where was I. Oh yes, Writing about the Temperance card.

```
I've always had a difficult time understanding
the Temperance card-number 14.
```

Chapter 15   The Devil

~ Misdirected Intentions ~

I hadn't been sleeping much, and now I'm just staring at a blank screen as I try to finish this chapter. Out of the dead silence, I suddenly hear a voice: "Hey, sleepy-head! Yeah, you."

I think I'm drinking too much coffee now for sure. It's amazing what the mind can do when exhausted.

"*Hey!* Down here!" Then I hear a shrill whistle!

I look down at my cards, and it seems like the Devil card is moving! He's waving an arm at me!

As I stare down at that card that's looking at me, the Devil says, "Do I have your attention now? You're awake, after all. I thought you were going to fall asleep right into your cup of coffee there."

I'm thinking, "This can't be happening," and then, as if reading my mind, he says, "Oh, yes it can, my friend. I figured it was about time you and I had a little chitchat," he says, with a grin.

Wow! I gasp, coughing out a cloud of cigarette smoke.

"Easy, friend, easy," he says. "You shouldn't be smoking those things, ya know. Bad for ya."

"What the hell do you care!" I blurt out to the card, and then I think, "What am I doing? I'm talking to a tarot card! I'd better get to bed."

"Well, they are bad for you—cigarettes, that is. And don't blame me for your bad habit. I had nothing to do with that," says the Devil as he pushes the ashtray toward me.

"But aren't you against all of mankind? My smoking should make you happy!"

"Actually I have nothing against mankind at all. I'm not a bad guy, once you get to know me. I'm a real angel, you know." He bats his eyes and gives me a big smile.

"Oh, the Devil is a comedian now too, huh? Well, don't quit your day job, pal," I say as I crush out the cigarette in the already-full ashtray.

"Well that's what gets my goat," he replies. "Excuse the pun. *Goat*—get it?" He winks. "I have been persecuted throughout the ages, and for what? Tell me one thing I did so bad to anyone."

"OK, how about tempting Jesus in the wilderness?" I say, leaning forward and pointing a finger right at him.

The Devil snaps back, "You're on, friend. Let me tell you how that all really went down—" he begins to say as he scratches his tail.

"And quit calling me *friend*!" I interrupt.

"Ooooh. Aren't we touchy today! OK, I'll call you ...Vince? Is that good for you?"

"Yes, I guess my name is OK. As long as you don't get my soul or anything by saying my name. You don't, do you?"

"Oh, please! I'm not into souls".

"So what really happened in the wilderness, then?" I ask. "As if you're going to convince me of anything. Please go ahead and give it your best. This will be fun to hear you squirm out of."

"I bet you I can convince you my intentions were good ones," he replies as he stands up quickly, pointing a finger at me.

"*Ha!*" I howl back. I'm getting comfortable talking with this card. "What you wanna bet me? Oh, let me guess—my soul? Not a chance, friend.

"Drop the soul thing, will ya? I hear that so much. I have absolutely no desire for your soul. What am I gonna do with a soul, anyway—sell it on eBay?

Let's get this straight, Vince: I don't collect souls. That was put on me years ago, and not true at all. Only you can control your soul. More bum wrap. How about we wager just a handshake? Or are you afraid to shake my hand?"

"Hell no, I'm not afraid! Your just a tarot card! And I'm just imagining this whole thing anyway, so you got a bet!" as I reach out for his hand to shake.

We shake hands, and he smiles at me as he begins explaining the whole wilderness thing with Jesus.

"First off," the Devil starts, "I was just trying to help make the world a better place. As you can see from what it is now, I didn't succeed."

"*Ha!* The Devil trying to make the world a better place. I'm sure you'll be considered for the Nobel Peace Prize."

"OK, OK—look, the very first thing I offered Jesus was to turn stone into bread, right? Of course your *black book* calls it 'tempting,' not 'offering', but either way, that was the first thing I asked Jesus about, right?"

"Well, yes from what I remember, yes. And he told you 'Man does not live by bread alone'" I answer.

"That's right, that's what he said. But if he could turn stone into bread, he could have fed the masses! No more starvation! Isn't that a good thing? I thought it was, but nooooo. I was a bad angel for offering that."

"OK, OK. Maybe Jesus just didn't trust you—probably would have been stale bread, anyway."

"OK—how about the second offer I made him? I told him if he were to honor me, all the kingdoms of the world would be his."

"No, you told him to *bow down* before you, and all the kingdoms of the world would be his," I reply.

"OK, maybe I got a little dramatic there—but all the kingdoms of the world? Come on! I think a little respect might have been in order, even if he is the boss's son. And if he had all the kingdoms of the world, guess what that would mean?" he asks.

I answered back, looking blankly, "Wha—?"

Leaning toward me, and looking into my eyes, he says, "No more war! That's what! If you own everything, who are you gonna pick a fight with?"

"Well, you gotta point there ... I guess," I say to him, scratching my head.

"Thank you very much!" the Devil snaps back with a pompous grin.

"OK, continue on, Mr. D. What about the last temptation, or offer, as you put it?"

"Well, I suggested that Jesus cast himself from the high place we were standing on down to the rocks below, knowing that the angels would swoop down and snatch him up before he hit bottom."

"So what's that gonna prove?" I snap back.

"So what?" he says. "So what? Well, the people would have seen that great spectacular thing happening, right?"

"Yeah, I guess so."

"OK," he continues, "OK, here is why that would be a good thing. If the people saw the angels come out of the sky, swoop down, and catch Jesus before he hit the rocks and then place him back up on the high place, wouldn't that be better than the air show in Chicago!"

"Yes that would be something to see. So you just wanted a little entertainment, then?"

"No!" says the Devil. "If the people see, with their own eyes, the angels do such a fantastic thing like that for Jesus, then all would know that he was the true son of God. No more doubt. Everyone in the world would be Christian after that happened. No other religions, which means no bitterness between one religion and another. And no more war based on religion, either. All would be on the same page.

"So Vince, let's review this whole thing about the three temptations in the wilderness. OK—first turn stone into bread, which equals lots of bread to eat for starving people. Second, owning all the kingdoms of the world means peace on earth. No wars. Third, everyone would know beyond a doubt the Jesus was the true son of God, and there would be only one true religion to follow because of it.

"Now, don't you think the world might have been a better place if he had taken me up on my offers?"

"Well," I say to card number fifteen. "Maybe you did get a bum wrap. I'll try to keep that in mind when you come up in my readings, OK? Fair enough?"

"Fair enough," says the Devil.

"Oh, Mr. D., one more thing."

"Yes?" he answers.

"I'm almost out of cigarettes; can you turn this empty pack into a full pack for me?"

"Now, you're the comedian Vince. Don't you quit your day job!" With that, the card becomes still again—a frozen image, just as before this conversation, and I think to myself, "*Wow!* That was some visualization I just had! I better get to sleep. One more smoke, and then off to bed." As I go to shake out my last cigarette in the pack, I see the pack is full. It's a brand-new pack of smokes! Well, now—I guess I do owe the Devil!   Thanks, Mr. D., and goodnight.

Chapter 16   The Tower

The ghost of Tom Joad

I decided to take a road trip down RT.66 just to see where I would end up. No plans, just drive. Gonna be gone for a week or so, I guess. I like to do that now and then.

No schedule. No dates to think about. Just go. I got out of the city and was just enjoying the open road for hours. Not even sure what state I'm in now. A clear night and the only light on the road is coming from my headlights on this lonely highway.

"Doesn't anyone drive a car around here?" I thought to myself. Well I guess it is late. Looks like something up ahead over that ridge. A motel with a lone gas pump right in front. A *Sinclair Ethyl Gasoline* sign hanging from one corner off the top of the pump.

I pulled into the small motel for the night. The VACANCY sign was dimly blinking off and on with the V not lit at all. *ACANCY... ACANCY.... ACANCY.* A good place for me to stop for the night. One dim light through a dirty window is still on in the office.

Hope this place is open. The door wasn't locked and I walked into a place that seemed lost in time. I see an old night clerk leaning across the lobby counter talking with two other old guys playing cards at a table centered in the small foyer.

Everyone stops and looks at me like I'm some novelty that just walked in the room! I look at them all looking at me and said…."HI!" The night clerk nodded back a silent *"Hello"* as he put both hands down on the counter and stood a little straighter while the two playing cards just kept staring in silence.

I heard one of the card players say *"The Highway's Alive Tonight."* I'm thinking….alive? There's nobody here! I walked up to the front desk and ask "Can I get a room?"

The clerk pushed up one sleeve on his frayed grey sweater and licks a pencil tip as he looks at the empty guest list in front of him. Without looking up he says "Name?"

"Vince" I answered.

He carefully wrote the five letters to the word VINCE on his guest list, turned around and pulls one of the keys off the wall behind him, puts it on the counter and says "That will be three dollars. Room 9. Check out time 10am. "Three dollars! Really?! I paid him and looked at the key he placed on the counter. A skeleton key! On a key ring attached it read " *Mother Road Motor Lodge. Where you can find all the comforts of home on RT66.*

Stamped on the key was a number 9. I looked at my watch and it read 2am. From the card table behind me someone says "You want some coffee?" I turned around and see the one old guy wearing a greyish white tee shirt and faded coveralls with a fedora hat tilted on his head leaning back in his chair pointing to the corner where there's a coffee pot simmering and some old cups hanging on the wall.

 "Yeah, thanks" I said as I walked over to the coffee pot and grabbed one of the cups.

I talked with the three old timers for awhile as I sipped on that coffee. The second fellow at the card table was wearing a blue denim shirt, work pants and a baseball cap pulled down low over his eyes. He never seemed to look up from his cards. Even when he spoke so I couldn't see much of his face.

I asked about the town as I looked out the window and saw an old water tower in a field across the road. "That's an old water tower isn't it?" I said

"Oh out there, yes. I think it's a water tower. Not used anymore though. Don't know why they don't knock it down. Probably cost too much to remove all that stone work." said the one in overalls as he draws a few cards to his hand.

"Yeah, I see windows in it. You ever go in there?" I asked.

"Not me. How bout you Sammy." he asked his friend who's putting 15 cents in the pot and said "Raise a nickle"

"You ever been in that old tower? " asking his friend again. His friend looks out from under his baseball cap and says "Nah. There's nothin in there." Then he turns in my direction and says "You're not from around here are ya?"

"No, Chicago." I answered.

"Chicaga. Long ways off. What brings ya out this way?"

"Ah, just lookin around." I answered.

"What, there nothin to look at in Chicaga? Gotta come all the way out by us to find somethin to look at? Well you got a good look at that water tower didn't ya? Ha ha!" as I see a big grin come out from underneath the brim of that baseball cap.

"Yeah, I did. You think I could go in there?" I asked as I looked out the window.

"What the tower? Don't see no reason why not. Nothin in there though. Might be locked up." said the desk clerk.

"You think someone in town gotta key to get in?" I asked.

"Sheriff might have a key if it needs one."replied the clerk

"Where's that at? The Sheriff's station." I asked.

"Oh Stan isn't there right now. He closes up around 6pm. Won't be back until the morning." replied the desk clerk as he took off his frayed grey sweater and hung it carefully on the wall.

"Ya means the Sheriff's station is closed for the night?" I asked.

"That's right. Ol' Stan locks it up around 6. You can call him at home but I wouldn't do that now just for a key to that old tower. I'm sure he's sleepin." said the clerk.

"Ya think I could just walk over there and look around?" I asked

That brought a smirk to all their faces as they looked at each other thinking why in the world would you want to walk around an empty field in the middle of the night to look at some old broken down water tower?

"Sure!" said the clerk. "No one gonna stop ya from walkin round in a field." He said as he grinned at his friends. "If that's what ya wanna do…go ahead and walk around in a field."

"Thanks" I said as I grabbed my key and walked out the door with my cup of burnt black coffee.

Without looking up from his cards, the old guy in the baseball cap says "Have fun walkin round in the field." and I heard them all start laughing as I walked out the door.

As I walked across that empty highway into the high grass toward that water tower I could hear the crickets chirping and see the lightening bugs flying in the quiet night air making that old tower even more curious looking. Like it doesn't belong there. Seems out of place in this setting.

As I got closer to the tower I almost tripped over an old set of railroad tracks hidden in the high grass. When I reached that old structure I just stood there looking at the stone work of that building for awhile.

Looks like a castle tower. The ground surrounding it was void of the high grass and laid with gravel years ago making the fabulous structure stand out even more ominous. As I stood there looking at all this, I notice a clearing off to my left and I saw a small fire in the dark.

"Is that a camp fire?" I think as I walk toward the small flickering light. As I get closer I see a man hunched over the fire stirring something cooking in a small pot over the flame. He wears a grey wool jacket and a dark fedora hat. On his feet were old work boots that were wide open with no laces. As I slowly approached him I heard him say *"The Highway is alive tonight."*

Then he looks in my direction and says "I gotta extra bowl if you like some soup. Trade ya for that coffee you're holding."

"Sure". I said.

As I sat down next to him by that fire he put out his hand and said "Name's Tom." I shook his hand and said…"Vince." He gave the soup a stir and said "There used to be a lot of us back here in the day. The Dust Bowl and all. Those was some shaky times"

As he poured some of the soup into a tin bowl he continued "This location was a shanty town back then. Places to sleep made out of anything you could get your hands on. Tar paper, card board boxes, pieces of wood, blankets..whatever. That tower was our marker."

I look around as he handed me the hot tin bowl and I gave him my coffee. I noticed a few old cars hidden in years of weeds and high grass.

"Wow is that a Model T over there." I asked. "Yeah" he says. "That was Miss Janet's automobile. She came driving in here to that motor lodge with white smoke barreling out of that Ford. The engine was a gonner. She couldn't afford to buy no oil. That sidevalve 4-cylinder was burnt out to nothin.

Miss Janet had no where to go, didn't know what to do. With her five year old son and all. She walked over here and we all did what we could for her and her boy. There was about 12 families here.

Mrs. Gains made a cup of tea for the woman and had a cup of warm milk for her boy with a spoonful of honey in it. Mr. Collins pulled out a pear from his pocket, cut it in half and shared one half with the boy.

Every night we all gathered around a big kettle of water boiling over a fire right here at this water tower. This was our meeting place. Everybody tried to add something to the soup kettle if they had it. A potato, celery, tomato. Jack Cooper had salt that he added to the pot every night.

This was like our little community. Freights used to come through here on that track back there. Some drifters would hop on a rail car and go, some drifters would be jumping off to stay awhile. The water tower was a marker for all who knew about this place.

This tower was where you walked off the road or jumped off the train. Ya looked for that tower and ya knew that was home for awhile.

I looked over at that model T and asked " What happened to Miss Janet and her little boy? "

 "I don't know. I hopped a freight about a week after she got here. Few months later I come back, she wasn't around and that was that. Hope they found a home somewhere." he said.

"Yeah .. me too." I said looking back at that Model T. I walked over to look into what was left of that rusted out relic. Nothing in there but a kids sock stuck to the back seat floor next to a broken car door handle.

I drank the rest of my broth, wiped the bowl clean with my bandana, handed it back to Tom and said "Thanks for the soup. Nice talkin with ya"

He handed me back my empty cup and said "See ya next time friend."

"Yeah sure" I said but I thought in my mind I don't think I'll be back. I went back to my Wrangler before going to my room for the night. Sitting in my jeep, I lit a smoke and tried to keep my eyes open after a long day on the road. So peaceful here. I closed my eyes and thought about the man at the campfire I was just talking with. Said his name was Tom....That was the last thing I remember.

 I woke up in the morning and realized I slept in the front seat of my car all night! Looked at my watch. 10am. Wow I slept here all night!

I got out and walked over to the motel. The front door was now just an empty entrance and the windows were all broken.

I walked in and went to the counter where I checked in last night. The whole place was covered in a thick layer of dust. Looks like no ones been in here for years. Then I noticed a stiff dry rotted grey sweater hangin on the wall behind the counter. I remember that was where the clerk hung up his sweater last night. I saw a broken down table resting on a tilt on the lobby floor with two broken chairs laying on their sides next to it.

I walked back out to my jeep thinking "What is this place?" As I opened my car door I noticed an old keychain on the ground half buried in the dirt.

I picked it out of the dirt and read the words *Mother Road Motor Lodge. Where you can find all the comforts of home on RT66* stamped on the keychain with a number 9 forged into the key itself.

I looked over at that motel one last time. Then over at that water tower in the field as I started my engine and drove off the lot back onto RT 66. After a few hours on that highway I reached for my cigarettes on the dash. But I noticed they fell onto the floor. Reaching down to get them with one hand still on the wheel I saw they were right next to an old coffee cup laying there in all the other junk on the floor. Where did this come from I thought as I quickly grabbed my smokes and the cup.

As lit a smoke I looked at that cup. Stamped on the cup was *Mother Road Motor Lodge Where you can find all the comforts of home on RT66*.

As I drove down that lonely road I thought maybe I'll come back when the highway is alive again. I'll just look for that old water tower. Tom said that's the marker. Maybe meet up with him again. I'll bring a few potatoes for the community pot just in case.

Then I remembered where I heard that saying before *"The Highway is alive tonight"* From the song *"The ghost of Tom Joad"* by Bruce Springsteen! Tom Joad was the main character in *The Grapes of Wrath by John Steinbeck!*

Nice talkin with ya Tom.

Chapter 17   The Star

Swing on a Star

It was a beautiful night so I decided to take a stroll around town. It's late enough where things are quieted down. I can think about things.

Sometimes I feel like I'm missing out on something. Don't know what it is though. Maybe I'll just let my mind drift and see if any new ideas come from the peaceful surroundings of this night stroll.

Tonight I decided to take a different route than usual. New scenery might spark new insight for me. A different path.

The Star card has been on my mind as we come to the end of the year. 2017 has past quickly with no new direction or plans taking hold in any significant way making me feel anxious for something. But what? What am I missing? Where am I going? Sometimes not having answers to those questions makes me feel lost.

I find myself entering into a park I didn't know was there. The walkway is nice and peaceful as I go deeper into this quiet park. A peaceful place for sure.

Up ahead I see a woman kneeling next to a small patch of water from this afternoons rain. She has long blonde hair and wears a blue sash that drapes over one shoulder. She holds an urn in each hand with one dipped into the water in front of her and the other pouring water out unto the ground at her side.

A young woman all by herself kneeling on the ground playing around with a puddle of water? At this time of night?! The night sky is clear and the stars and moon shine brightly as I realize it's The Star card right before me!

As I walk past her she says "Nice night. Wouldn't you agree?"

I stopped and replied "Yes, it is. I know you. You're the Star card."

Yes you could call me that. Although I have had other names over time."

As she continues pouring water unto the ground she started singing.
 🎵 *"Would you like to swing on a star.* 🎵
 🎵 *Carry moonbeams home in a jar.* 🎵
  🎵 *And be better off than you are.* 🎵

"Hey I know that song! *Swinging on a star*,
That's an old song!" I said.

"I know, and the words are so true." she said as she looked down at the trails of water being made as she slowly emptied the urn out onto the dry ground at her side.

"You've always been a curious card to me." I said

 "And why is that Vincent?"

"You know my name?" I said.

"I know you as well as you know me." She answered back

"Wow! Neat. I always think of you representing direction. Do you feel that's what you're about?.....Direction?" I asked

"Sometimes yes. Sometimes I can be seen as something distant too. Or seen as a sign. Or something to make a wish upon or even something as subtle as a twinkle in your eye. But yes, I can be seen as a guiding light as well. But remember once you see that guiding light you have to keep your eyes peeled as you move forward. New paths are not clearly marked. That's where some people run into problems and get lost. " She said as she poured more water unto the ground.

"Why do you do that? Pour that water on the ground I mean? That never made any sense to me. "

She looked up at me with a slight smile and said
"The water shows paths. The water travels randomly in various directions. Water always takes the easiest path forward."

"The path to accomplishment is usually the hardest path to take. We can become confused as the easiest path is always the one we see first. That path is the most clear in our minds but not always the wisest choice."

"These smaller winding paths of water could be showing the right path to take. Having the most rewards. It can show accomplishment that might seem hidden until we look closely." She said as she pointed to the smaller watery lines in the dirt.

"Wow, OK.
Well do you see anything for me in that dirty water?
Sometimes I feel a little lost." I asked as I gazed into her little pond of water flowing out in all different directions.

"You're not lost Vincent. You can't be lost if you don't have any idea where you want to go. And you don't have a clue on that right now. You have no focused destination."

"How do I find that focused destination?" I asked.

She looked up at me and said "Ah. You need to yearn for something. You need to crave something. When you want something bad enough that you can taste it, then you have a path to follow."

She poured more of the water and continued "You don't know what you want to do anymore. That brings about a sense of having no direction in your life. You need to figure out your next passion. You've had many so it shouldn't be that hard for you Vincent. Passions are a gift. Some people don't have any passions in their life. They just move along from one day to the next. But you've been rich with passion. Find your passion at this time in your life. That will bring about your next direction."

"Wow, I haven't thought about that stuff lately." I said

"Oh you have Vincent. It bothers you whether you think about it or not. It's a haunt. You need something to thirst for."

"Write another book?" I asked.

"Maybe. You have to figure that out yourself. Only you can find your direction Vincent. And then you can have the joy of feeling lost as you search for accomplishing that passion in you. That fire."

"The joy of feeling lost?!" I asked.

"Yes that curious joy. The joy of wonder. The joy of trekking into untraveled territory." she said with a smile.

"Yes Vincent, you're searching for it now. You just have to think clearly about it. You get too anxious. You're like the dog chasing a car. That is exciting to you. Actually it can be exciting to anyone who experiences it. Your direction is not a physical location. It is a frame of mind. Wanna hint Vincent?"

"Yeah. Sure!" I said.

"Reaching a pinnacle is the key to your path Vincent. That's what you want most. What gives you the feeling of ultimate accomplishment? That one thing will be your next passion. You love to chase what has never been caught before Vincent. Like an archeologist discovering an ancient tomb for the first time."

That's when I heard a voice from behind say "Sir?"
I turned around to a bright light flashing right in my eyes.
What are you doing here Sir?"

As the light points down from my eyes I see a police officer standing there with a flashlight.

"Uh. Hi officer!" I said.

"I asked what are you doing here Sir?" He said again.
"This park closes at 10pm."

"Uh Oh! I didn't realize it was that late officer."

"You don't know what time it is?" he said. "This park closed hours ago Sir. Have you been drinking?"

"No, what would make you think I was drinking officer?"

"Well you're standing here in a closed park in the middle of the night having a conversation with that mud puddle. You need to show me some identification Sir."

I look back at that Star Maiden who has a smirk on her face as she knows the police officer doesn't see her. She wags a finger at me as if saying bad boy! Then she laughs.

"Uh, well Officer, uh, I didn't bring my wallet with me. Ya see I was just taking a walk and uh, well, I wasn't planning on buying anything or ..... anything. Ya know. Everything is closed this time of night." I said as I kicked the ground a little.

"You live near here Sir?"

"Uh, not really sure Officer. I got a little turned around here and not sure where I am right now.....Officer. Is this Berwyn? I live in Berwyn. This is still Berwyn right?" I asked hoping it was.

"No you're in Riverside right now. Berwyn is the next town over."

The star card lady is just staring at us both with a smile.
" You seem very interested in that mud puddle Sir. Can you tell me why?" he asked as he flashes the light unto the puddle of water, obviously not seeing the Star Maiden.

"Oh no! Im not interested in that mud puddle at all officer. I'll just be going now..... Uh.... nice talking with you sir and thanks for letting me know that the park closes at 10pm. I will make a note of it. Hate to walk around here after hours ya know..... You have a wonderful evening officer." I said as I started to walk away.

Then he yelled out to me. "Hey!"

I stopped in my tracks and turned slowly around to face him and said…."Yes?"

"Berwyns' that way" as he pointed in the other direction.

"Oh thanks officer" I said as I looked back towards the direction I was walking. "But I think I'm just gonna keep going this way for awhile. All those stars out tonight look so good to me. So vast. So many."

As I looked up into the night sky I started thinking. Each star looks like an opportunity of discovery. Life has so many possibilities to choose from. So many paths that can be taken. Which one to choose is the key question. Once you see that, it just becomes a matter of reaching for that one star. I'm gonna search for that special star tonight. That one star that seems just a little out of my reach. That's the one I want.

I gave one last glance back to the Star Maiden giving her a nod and a smile. As I walked away I could hear her singing that old song from the 1940's again.

♪ *Would you like to swing on a star….* ♪
♪ *Carry moonbeams home in a jar…* ♪
♪ *And be better off than you are…* ♪
♪ *You could be better than you are…..* ♪
♪ *You could be swinging on a star….* ♪

Chapter 18   The Moon

The Tower on the right

As I sit here writing about the Moon card I think to myself, what a mysterious card.
Number 18 sure is lonely looking. No people in there at all. Just those two mysterious looking towers in the middle of the night.

Oh well, I don't have time to think about every little detail of each card anyway. I'm writing a book not an encyclopedia set.

As I get up and go into the kitchen to get another glass of wine I hear crickets and I notice the floor isn't tile anymore. It's grass and the room is filled with a thick cloudy misty fog. "Whoa! Where the hell am I!" As I try to feel my way to the refrigerator two dogs come out of the fog and start circling around me sniffing my robe. "HEY!!!"

One grabs my sleeve and starts pulling. *"Hey Let Go!"*
He just growls as he keeps tugging. *"HEY LET GO!!"*
I yelled out as the other dog starts snarling like crazy.

The next thing I know I step into a damn creek! "Whoa! What's going on here! — Where are you taking me!" I yelled out as a big ass crawfish almost takes off one of my toes!

"Wow! I'm in the damn card! The Moon card! Number 18! Here I am! There are those two towers up ahead and the one on the right has a light on in the window."

"OK, OK I get it doggie. Nice doggie. Let go, I'll follow. Good doggie." The other dog is still snarling at me as we slowly walk toward that tower with the lit window. He's watching every move I make as we get closer. "Gooood doggie." I try to give him a pet but he gently snaps at my hand, just missing it. "OK! Geez!"

Once we're in front of the old tower the dogs sit. One on each side of the archway entrance. Panting with tongue's out looking at me. Then they both start howling.

The tower is about 80 feet high and 30 feet wide. All stone. "This place sure is old." Thinking to myself as I ring out my wet robe. Wow. The stars are bright and that moon is full. The crickets are sure loud enough and I can still hear the water flowing over the rocks of the creek I stepped into.

I start to see a light flashing from inside. It's moving from side to side as it comes down a staircase. As it gets closer I can hear foot steps along with the clinking of keys.

Then someone grumbles. *"Who's there?"*

"Uh, hello?" I answered to let him know I'm there as he flashes a flashlight in my face.

A short, bald, overweight man with a pale complexion asked "Who are you?" He was wearing a white security guard shirt and holding a jelly roll in his left hand. His mouth was sugar coated and a dab of red cherry jelly was on the front of his white shirt. What a slob!

"Uh, I'm Vince." I said

"How'd you get in here?" He asked.

"I don't actually know." I said. "I was just going to my kitchen to get another glass of wine and the next thing I know I'm this dogs *chew toy!* — Uh.... you got some jelly— on your shirt." I tried to say as politely as I could. "Is this still Berwyn?" I asked.

"Berwyn?" he says.

"What's Berwyn?" he says as he chews away on that jelly roll.

Looking back towards the creek I said "Its where I live."

"Oh. Well follow me to my office and will get you registered."

" Oh thanks but I just wanna get back to my kitchen." I say to him as I point back toward the creek not knowing where else to point.

"Yeah— follow me". The dogs start to follow and he yells out "FRIC! Stay! FRAC go on now boy. Go!" As one of the dogs trots back into the dark night the other lays down by the entrance. We walk up the long skinny staircase with just his flashlight for direction.

At the top of the staircase we come to his office, a dimly lit room with a cluttered desk including a box of those stupid jellyrolls.

"Want some coffee"? He asked as he points to the almost empty coffee pot simmering away on the burner.

 I grab a cup and wiped it clean with my wet robe. "You ever wash these things?" I asked?

"No" he said. "Don't get much company here anymore."

"Why's that?" I asked as I took a sip of the thick burnt coffee.

"People are too busy being busy I guess." he says as he looks through his mess on the desk. "What your name again?" as he looks through his papers?

"Uh, Vincent Pitisci. From Berwyn." I answered watching him shuffle through his papers.

"Oh yes, here you are. *Vincent Pee tee shee*, from Birwin. Says here you're an author. That true?"

"Well yes sir, I am." I answered back

"Says here you wrote a book on the Tarot cards. That true?"
 He said—Looking at me over his bifocals.

"Yes sir. It is." I replied

"Says here *Genius of the Tarot* — You a genius then?" he asked.

"No sir, the Tarot is genius — not the author. That's just the title." I explained, hoping that this won't take too long.

"You're late, you were scheduled to be here last week." He said looking at a calendar on the wall.

"I was? " I said looking at him with surprise.

"Yes you —*was*." he said. "That's ok, no harm done. I'm free now. So what you wanna know about the *Moon card?*"

"What? Really? Well everything you can tell me. Yes everything! Who else is here besides us?"

"No one, the place is empty. All sorts of interesting stuff to look at though if you wanna go upstairs. Many spirits here too."

"Who works the other tower?" I asked looking out the window.

"No one now. They let Joey go a few years back. Business has been slow so it's just me, FRIC and FRAC."

"The dogs?" I asked,

"Yes the security dogs. They're good boys they are."

"How about that big crawfish in the creek? Is that a security crawfish too?" I asked.

"Huh? No, that's just a crawfish." He chuckled. — *security crawfish* he says to himself with a grin as he shakes his head while writing in his note book.

"What's down past these towers?" I asked. "Anything interesting?"

"Of course." he said. "Your path is that way."

"It is?"

"Course it is." He replied

"Is it dangerous?" I asked.

"Yes, he said. if you're not careful, yes it is.
So watch your ass out there. The dogs will only take you to the end of these towers. After that you're on your own son. Have a jelly roll son. Help kill the taste of that burnt coffee."

"Thanks, I think I will. So what's in store for me down my path then mister?"

"What your looking for?"

"Not sure." I said.

"You better be sure before you take that trek son. You better know real good what it is you want before you start out. Once you pass these towers there's no turning back this way again. Only forward."

"Wow— hey mister, I think I might have made a mistake. I was just going into my kitchen to get a glass of wine and I ended up here in the *Moon card!* I wasn't ready for this."

"Oh you're ready son, you just don't know it yet. Afraid? Opportunities don't come that often."

"Well kinda— yes. Besides I'm just in a wet bathrobe and my wallet's in my pants in the apartment and my cigarettes are on the desk and uh, well I would have to let people know I'm going somewhere too.
 And I got some.... readings I have to do... tomorrow so I can't leave yet, …..ya know?"

"Your body doesn't go anywhere new. It's a change in your frame of mind son. That's all. You'll still be in your little town of *Biiirwiiin*. But you'll be a different person once you take that path. — You ready?"

"Uh, no! Not yet, OK? Uh, can I call ya when I'm..... ready? Uh, still got some things to do around the place and Uh, well, uh, ya know, stuff."

"Its a wonderful path son, once you got the guts to take it."

"Well you mind if I just go back to my kitchen for now? Besides I gotta finish my next book."

"Don't you wanna see what's upstairs? Or the other tower? These towers hold many secrets just waiting to be discovered. People just have to take that path and go through those cold dark doors. Mystery. The unknown. Enchantment beyond your wildest dreams. But only once you decide to break away from the norm. People don't have what it takes to venture out and live their lives anymore. Everyone just conforms to the status quo. Like I said, it's been slow around here."

"Uh, no thanks but thanks anyway. Uh can I get back home from here?"

"Sure you can. Just walk through that door again. Same one you came in from. It leads right to your kitchen."

"Really?! Thanks! Uh, See ya. I'll call soon."

"Sure you will son."

I said Bye as I walked back through the door. Then I saw the fluorescent light of my kitchen! I hear my refrigerator running and I felt the cold tile floor on my feet! "I'm back! Thank God! Wow!" Shaking, I poured myself a glass of that cool wine from my fridge. "Home sweet home!

I better splash some water on my face and regroup." As I look into my bathroom mirror I see sugar all over my mouth and looking down I see red cherry jelly on the front of my wet robe. "Wow did I just throw away an opportunity?"

I remember he said, *'You better be sure before you take that trek son.'* Hope I get another chance once I know the direction I want to take. Maybe I could be the security guard on the left tower! Would be a great place to write! Maybe someday even go beyond those towers. Until then, tonight I'll sleep in my bed here at home.

Maybe someday— I said to myself, holding my glass of wine, sitting in my chair........as I drifted off into sleep.

Chapter 19 The Sun

Appreciated

Thought it was time to write about the Sun card of the Major Arcana. As I sit there wondering, I think to myself...Is it hot in here or what. Maybe I'll open a window, turn on the fan.

Then I hear someone say "Hello sunshine."

I look behind me and see a big bright yellow face wearing sunglasses floating there in the room! Wow!

 "Are you the Sun???!!!"

"In the flesh Vincent– Or maybe I should say...In the *'hydrogen, oxygen, carbon, nitrogen, magnesium, iron and a little silicon."*

I just stared trying to shield my eyes from the brightness. "Can you turn that down a little. You're hurting my eyes."

"Sure Vince, how's this? " he said as the room dimmed to a nice level.

"A lot better, Thanks. Hey I'm happy to meet you." I said

"Yes, I do have a tendency to brighten up people's days don't I?
I'm glad you're writing about me Vincent. This is exciting!" he replied

"Really? Writing a couple of pages in a book about you excites you?" I said

"You're the SUN. You've been recognized by many throughout mankind's history. Even worshiped!"

"Ah yes, the good ol days.
But no one ever really talks to me anymore. It's just like...OK....the sun is out. I don't get as much attention as I used to get. They're too busy to be thinking about me today. People need to get outside more. No one thinks I'm a big deal anymore. So this conversation is a nice change."

"Well I'm glad to hear it. What should I call you anyway?"

"The Sun." he said with a blank look.

"Oh, well yeah, I guess that would work." I said.

"Did you know that I was your first god?" he asked
I mean even before Shiva, Buddha, Jesus, Isis, Well all of them."

"Yeah I guess you were."

"I mean I am life giving. And I am the light. I give you warmth, breath, things that grow for you to eat. I give you light and protect you against the darkness. And it's very rewarding to me too. "

"It is?"

"Yes."

"Well you're a hot item that's for sure." Ha!

"Yes, about 30 million degrees F. Give or take." said the Sun

"Wow, that's hot!"

Yes, but it's a dry heat Vincent."

Hey, if you're that hot how come those sunglasses you're wearing aren't melting."

"Are you kidding Vincent? These are *RayBans*, They're too cool to melt."

"Hey, are you God?" I asked

"Well lets just say you will understand more as time goes on my friend."
"uh-huh, OK."

"Well I think you are what we perceive as God."

He smiles a big grin.
"They even named glasses after me."

"They did?"

"Sure....SUN..glasses!
And all your movie stars always wear them."

"So, when I come up in those Tarot cards what do you think it means Vincent?"

"Well always good news." I said.
"Nurturing situation, bright future, things seen clearly. New life on a goal.
Centering on issues of concern."

"Well Vincent, how about many opportunities all around you hidden in plain sight. Answers that are so close to you that you don't see them. You live in a perfect environment and I am all around you. Everywhere you look, Even at night, I'm close by. Life giving that is so vital you can't imagine being without it. Things kept in order, a good foundation, planned movement, cycles, one of many." said the Sun

"How do you mean one of many?" I asked

"Come on Vincent. Carl Sagan? Billions and billions– remember?"

"Oh yeah. Carl Sagan. He was one of your biggest fans."

"But I do like your idea of centering too Vincent."

"Well if it weren't for you all the planets, including mother earth here would just fly out into deep space. Right? No centering?" I said.

"Yes, and its a little chilly out there in deep space Vincent."

"How chilly?" I asked

"About 450 degrees below zero Vincent.
So if you decide to go outside of my area you better bundle up."

"I'm not planning leaving anytime soon." I said.

"Me either." said the Sun.

"Good. We need you here. You can come by anytime." I said

"Good. I'll see you tomorrow."

"I hope so." I said as he faded away.

Chapter 20   Judgement

A Wake Up Call

BLAAAARRRRE!!!!

Whah! What was that!!!!!

BLAAAARRRE!!!!!!

Holy smokes! Where's that coming from!
Sounds like a train horn right next door!

BLAAAARRRE!!!!!!

"OK OK STOP!"

That's when I hear someone say — *"Good morning Vincent"*

"Who said that?!"

BLAAAARRRE!!!!!!

"Whoa! Stop that!!"
I yell out as I look at my alarm clock —5AM and I see my Tarot deck right next to it. Then I look up and see the Angel of Judgment is standing right by my bed looking at me.

"You like my trumpet?" — he says as he brings that horn to his lips again.

"Wait!!! Don't blow that thing again please!!
I'm up OK? Jesus Christ! My ears are ringing." I said as I got out of bed.

"Did you just say — JESUS CHRIST!?" he says as he brings that horn back to his lips giving me a stern look.

"What? Uh —NO! I didn't say .... that name. Why, is that bad? I said Uh...... *'Heeee's So-Nice'* meaning you of course that is."

"Aahh, Thank you Vincent." He says with a smile

"Well you're welcome Sir, I mean…um….what should I call you... again?"

"Judgment is good but I do prefer Gabe." He said as he looked around my messy room.

"OK, Nice horn by the way. Works real good."
"Too good" I mumble to myself.
"Where did you get it?" I asked as I looked around for my cigarettes.

"Don't ask" — he says with a grin.
"How's the book coming?"

"Oh I don't know. It's coming along OK." I answered as I walked into the kitchen to get coffee.
 "Harder than I thought it would be— that's for sure.
 Being an author that is. Hope people like it."

"So you're concerned with others judging your book than?" He says, following me around my apartment as I keep looking for my cigarettes.

 "Well yeah, I'm kinda concerned, I guess."

"Don't worry about others judging your book Vincent.
Worry about how you judge it. That's the key.
You are the true judge of that book. You're the only critic you need to convince."

"That makes sense. Well I like it that's for sure. But I'm not gonna be blowing my own horn about it just yet. Oh wait! I didn't mean that!"

He just looked at me with a smile tapping his fingers on that big trumpet.

"It is your creation." he said. "No one will ever care more about that book than you. If you like it, you won't care what the rest of the world thinks of it. And if you truly believe in it, I believe others will too."

"You really think so!? — I hope so." I answered

"Don't hope —Know Vincent. Know you wrote the best book you possibly could before you release it. Then you can truly stand by it. So when you gonna write about me?" he asked with a curious look.

"Well I guess now that you've woke me up. Along with waking up the rest of the building with that horn."

"Don't worry, no one else heard that bugle blare but you.
You're the only one whose judging yourself lately.
Judging how your book is written that is. That's why you heard that trumpet blare. You want the recognition as an author. You want to blare your trumpet about your book. And that's fine and good Vincent."

"Do ya think I could borrow your horn when the book is completed?" I said, looking at his trumpet. "That would do the trick. I'll take care of it. Whadda ya think Judgement? I mean Gabe."

So you think my trumpet is louder than yours?" He said.
"Believe me Vincent, your trumpet will blare the loudest for you and only you. You just gotta find yours."

"Well where the hell is it then? Under the damn couch?! I don't have one of those things—let alone blow it." I replied, still looking around the room for my cigarettes.

"Did you just say — DAMN!?" he says as he brings that horn to his lips again.

"Wha—? NO! I said — HAM! You want some HAM? uh I'm just

gonna make a HAM sandwich and I got some HAM. You wanna sandwich— With some HAM?"

"You're starting to sound like *Dr. Seuss* Vincent.
But no thanks. I ate just before I came to see you.
Your trumpet is within you Vincent."

"Good" — I said to myself looking in the fridge. "*I don't have anymore ham in here anyway. Whew.* Uh, maybe I'll just make some toast later." I said as I poured some of yesterdays coffee from the pot.
"So Judgement Card, tell me all about yourself." I asked as I turned on my computer.

"I'm all about you Vincent. How do you judge yourself?"

"I'm OK"

"That's it? OK? What a wimp!" He laughed.

"Whaddya mean wimp?!! I said I was OK. What's so wimpy about OK? Why don't ya mind your own business."

"It is my business. I'm Judgment remember? So — Just OK?
You just looked into yourself and said *'Well I'm not the best. I have faults, weaknesses and all that but I guess — I'm OK.'*
People judge themselves too harshly Vincent.
So really, how's that book coming?"

"The book's not bad so far." I said

"That's it! You want people to read your book as say.. It's not bad? That's it?! And you say you're not a whimp!! It's Not bad?!
 'I read Vincent's book…it's not bad'. Ha!"

"Is there anything good about it? Now that we know – '*it's not bad.*' Is it good at all? Why don't you title your book '*The Tarot ~ This book is not bad by Vincent Pitisci.*' Or how about '*The Tarot ~ This book will do by Vincent Pitisci*'
 I got it! '*The Tarot ~ Reading this book won't hurt by Vincent Pitisci.*' And you want a trumpet?! Maybe a kazoo but you're not ready for a trumpet."

"Well Jesus Cri..."

"*Careful Vincent!*" As he brought that horn to his mouth again.

"Oh! Yeah, thanks, almost forgot.
Ya know what? You shouldn't be so '*Judgmental.*" I said using air quotes. "Maybe you outta look in the mirror instead of pointing fingers at everyone else."

And once I got going I couldn't stop.—"You want some judgment? I'll give ya some judgment. You're a boring Tarot card — ya know that? Boring! How's that for some judgment?! I never did like you."

Then I turned back around pointing a finger at him —"Oh — and another thing. I'm judging from my alarm clock that you woke me up too early. That was *bad judgment*. Now I'm *judging* that I'm still tired so I'm gonna *judge* myself back to bed now. Good bye!"

I turned off the light and got in bed.

"*Comes in my apartment bothering me like he owns the place Geez.*"

As I laid there trying to go back to sleep I felt something was poking me in the back. "What the hell is under here." I reach in the dark and grab a blunt hard piece of something. I turned the light back on to see what was in my hand... A Kazoo.

 toot!

Chapter 21   The World

Remember this one?

Sitting at my computer listening to new age music in the background always helped me to write. Peaceful background music is so nice. As I start to write about the World Card number 21 my computer starts to glitch out on me and my background new age music changed to some stupid big band era stuff. Sounded like *Glenn Miller*.

It is *Glen Miller. In the Mood!* What's this nonsense! As I try to fix my computer a flash of light followed by a blast of foggy smoke mushrooms up in my room!

As the fog clears away I see a woman right there in my room and she's dancing to the music. *In the mood!* And she's wearing nothing but a scarf and a *sneeze*!!!! "Who are you!!??" I say to the dancer.

"Who do ya think handsome?" She says as she turns and sways with that scarf.

"Hey, you're the *World Card* aren't you?" I say to her as I make the connection. "I get it, I'm writing about you so you decided to say Hi. Is that it?"

"Wow you are a genius after all Vinny. You mind if I call you Vinny? Your friends do don't they?"

"Some yes. Hey, you wanna robe or something?"

"No, I have more than enough scarf here to be modest." She says, wrapping the scarf around herself like a makeshift suri as she sways to the music

"Wanna dance Vinny?"

"What? No! I don't wanna dance. I'm writing here and this ain't no disco. Besides I haven't danced in years. Don't think I could anymore if I did try."

"Life's a dance Vinny. You start dancing the minute you rise in the morning."

"No I don't. I walk to the bathroom and then I walk to the kitchen sink and make coffee. That's not dancing. besides you need a partner to dance and I'm alone here. You need a partner unless you're some kinda kook or something."

"You shake a tail feather every day Vinny. You just don't know you're doing it, but others know. They see what you do and how you move. You dance, Vinny— its just not to music anymore. But you still got it handsome." She says as she grabs my hand.

"Hey! Cut it out lady —will ya. I'm not interested in *'Gotting it'!* I'm trying to finish writing this book."

"You dance with me every day Vinny. Every time you pick up those cards we dance. And you're pretty good at it I might add."

"Oh. well, I guess if you think of reading cards as dancing, well yes I guess I dance then. Just dancing sitting down that's all." I said as I heaved my chest out a little.

She leans over giving me a grin and says — "Remember this?"

I start to hear *I Get Around* by the *Beach Boys*

"OMG! Yes! I learned how to dance to that song! Neat! Wow does that bring back memories. Me and my buddy would practice dancing to that with his older sister. Wow."

"Go ahead Vinny... show me."

I couldn't resist making a spin and then started stepping to the music like I learned to back then.

"Wow! Yeah Vinny shake it up!" She said with a laugh.
Then the music changed to the *Beatles—Twist and Shout*.
That was it. I was gone as I started twisting and moving to the music.

Tighten Up by *Archie Bell and the Drells!* came next! Gosh I forgot that one —yes!

I started to do the *Tighten Up* and was moving across the floor to the music shifting my hips and sliding my feet.

The Four Tops – Bernadette came next. Gosh!

James Brown— Pappa's Gotta Brand New Bag! I couldn't help myself as I did the *James Brown*, getting into it now, gliding across the room with ease.

"You got it Vinny! Yes baby move it for me!" she said as she danced with me.

"You asked for it *Blondie*" and I did the splitz to end that *James Brown* tune.

As I got up, I noticed I was the only one in the room. My new age music was playing peacefully and my computer was showing nothing on the screen but the words *The World XXI*.

I sat down at my computer feeling a little silly imagining I could still dance. I must have looked ridiculous hopping around here like that. *Geez* — glad my drapes were closed.

I felt like I was moving with perfect stride to those old songs but I know if I had a movie camera of what just occurred it would look pretty sad for sure. Hell walking up and down the stairs hurts let alone dancing to music.

But in my heart I was dancing perfectly again. I had it better than ever! I felt it just like when I was a teenager.

I must have had too much wine. But it was fun to remember that feeling again. Time for bed. But tomorrow I will ask Lynda to dance with me, just for old time sake. Slowly of course. That would bring back that feeling again as well.

I went to bed and turned off the light and thought — *"Thanks for the dance Blondie."*

The Mona Lisa

YOU REALLY WANT TO KNOW?

Images can say many things even if they are not images of the Tarot. I keep a 11"x14" print of the *Mona Lisa* right by my computer. If you look at that picture you will see more than just that smile she is known for. Look into those eyes.

Geez— you can see there is much going on in that head of hers. Quietly thinking about more than she lets on. It's like she has to be still for the pose but her mind is going full tilt!

That's really what *DaVinci* captured in that painting. The action of thought. She has a look that says so much with so little effort, making that masterpiece more powerful than most would normally think at first glance. It's almost as if *DaVinci* has been able to paint thoughts from her mind without using images. I can see why she's such a classic.

I wonder what she was thinking at the time that face was captured by Leonardo.

"You really want to know?"

"Wha—?
Did you just say something?! — To me!!??" I say, looking at the picture.

"Do you see anyone else here?" She said, as she came to life with that smile.

"No." I answered

"*Well?....* She continued.

"But you're not a Tarot card." I replied.

"Is that a requirement?— To be a Tarot card?" she answered

"Why no—not at all. Welcome.
 Wow — The Mona Lisa! Visiting me! Wow! Gosh!"

"Hello to you Vincent" she politely said.

"The Mona Lisa visiting me!"

"You can just address me as Lisa — OK?"

"UH? Sure. Wow just Lisa. I'm just calling the Mona Lisa — Lisa."

"You wanted to know what I was thinking when the master was painting my portrait?"

"Yeah!! Sure! What?"

"My back was killing me!" she said. "Just sitting there for hours on end. It really did try my patience. But that was the case for anyone willing to have their portrait done."

"But you have this look like you're thinking about something so deep. So quietly curious." I said.

"Well you sit there all day long and see what kind of face you end up having. Curious looking? Well watching him work was a very curious sight. Yes I was full of curiosity at times." She said.

"Nothing to do but think. But yet not move. He demanded an expressionless pose. He said expressions change in a face too easily as the day moves on.

It was important to him that my expression not change but my mind was always going — yes.

I guess I was a little curious as to what the painting was looking like. I think I show my curiosity in that picture the most."

"Did he instruct you how to pose?" I asked curiously

"Well yes. He's the one doing the painting.
But he did take into consideration that I had to stay comfortable for hours at a time. So I look comfortable there."

"Why was the painting made?" I asked.

"It was my husbands idea."

"Oh?"

"Yes we were newly weds and he wanted my picture.
We didn't have cameras ya know."

"Is your husband with you now?"

"No we drifted apart over the ages of time."

"You wanna get married again?
The wedding pictures would be worth a fortune!!!! — Ha!"

"Is that a proposal?" she said with a smirk."

"Uh, well— would you accept if I asked you?"

"No — But I am curious about you just the same." she said with a grin.

"And why is that?" I asked.

She just smiled back at me with that famous look.

"Well — I'm curious about you too." I said.
"You want to go out to dinner or something?
I would be honored to take you."

"I think it best we just sit." she answered.
 "Although I always wanted to try a *Big Mac*.
 They look quite tasty."

"A Big Mac! *Geez* take the Mona Lisa out to dinner and we go to *McDonalds*. Ha!
 I can do that for you. *McDonalds* is right across the street.
 I eat there all the time ya know... I got clout over there —
  It's nothing for me to go over there and order a *Big Mac* anytime I want one. See— I even got coupons."

"I know. I see you eating *Big Macs* all the time."

"You do?"

"Of course I do. I've been sitting here on your table for over two years now."

"Hey — You wanna glass of wine?" I asked

"No thanks. I see you drinking that all the time too.
 Does everyone drink wine with *Big Macs*?" She said with a smirk

"Uh — No. What was it like to know *DaVinci*!?" I asked, changing the subject.

"He was a curious kook. Always talking to himself. I think he talked more with himself than he spoke to other people. He found himself to be quite interesting.

 He was curious about everything. He must have come up with twenty different ideas everyday while he was painting my portrait. Things just came into his head so quick. But they left just as quick as they came. So he was constantly writing things down before he lost his thoughts."

"Hey! I know what I wanna ask you!!!" I said.

"And what would that be Vincent?"

"Can you tell me about *DaVinci's* painting of the *Last Supper*?
 In it, the apostle standing next to *Jesus* on his right looks like a woman. Is it? Is it supposed to be *Mary Magdalene*?"

"Take a closer look at it Vincent.
 He had a whole portfolio of faces in his collection to use for paintings. He had many of me before doing my portrait."

"What's that gotta do with the *Last Supper* painting?" I asked.

"Who does that apostle you're asking about look like?" She said

"I don't know— *Hilary Clinton?*"

"No." She says as she adjusts her pose a little and looked at me again.

"NO! YOU? He used you for the person standing next to *Jesus* in the *Last Supper*!!!! OMG! YOU!
 He used the Mona Lisa in the Last Supper!!"

"He never said that to me but I have a feeling he used my face. I guess we'll never know for sure, will we? But you think about it.—

"So how's your book on Tarot cards doing?
 I enjoy Tarot cards." She said as she glanced over at my deck.

"You do? You read them then?" I asked

"Not in the same manner as you Vincent.
We would use them to tell poetic stories at gatherings.
 They were fun to play with."

"Cool! Tell me a story." I said as I passed my deck to her.

She looked at my cards for a full minute or so. Holding them and arranging them in her hands as if she is tapping into me instead of them.

Then she proceeded.

The first card she laid down was *The Hermit* and then she said —

*"I know him not — But yet I do
This man of vision and deep thought too."*

She looked up at me with a smile.
Then she put down a second card. It was *The Hanged Man*.
And she continued —

*"I know him not — But yet can see
A deep concern he tries to free."*

She looked up at me again only this time with a look of knowing something about me.

The third card she placed was *Temperance* and she spoke again —

*"I know him not — But I can tell
His light shines bright and his shadows fell."*

She gave a gentle smile my way
She was reading me.

Then she laid down another card — *The Magician* and she spoke

*"I know him not — But he shall know
the Tarot cards are in his soul."*

I felt her energy go right through me as she looked deep into my eyes.

And then she turned over a final card — *The Lovers* and with a playful smile she said

*"I know him not — But once in time
My love was his and his was mine."*

She laid the cards down quietly and looked at them for a moment. and then said with a smile— "So how did I do?"

I sat in awe. Then I said "That was a beautiful reading. That was a priceless reading. I don't know what it all meant but it sure sounded nice coming from you. You read Tarot cards as nicely as you pose for pictures. Thank you Lisa. "

"That was fun Vincent
OK — Your turn. Now you read me" She said with a grin.

"What? I can't read you. You're the Mona Lisa! How am I gonna read you?"

"Well you're the pro. You should be able to read me." She said with a slight chuckle

"Well I can't."

"Are you chicken?" she said and started to laugh.

"Yeah" I replied right back

She laughed more saying "You're really chicken aren't you?". She was really laughing. I made the Mona Lisa laugh! Ha!. I saw her teeth! I saw the Mona Lisa's teeth! Wow!

"I enjoyed our little chat Vincent.
But I really must be going now anyway— It was nice talking with you. Good luck with your book. I hope it is a successful venture."

"Hey! Wait a minute! Come on — I'll get you a *Big Mac* if you stay awhile more! Hey!"

I just stared at the picture waiting for it to come back alive again. And she just stared back motionless but with that look in her eyes as if she was still here with me.

Like she's still here only now not moving. Just looking. Just thinking. I'm gonna put a *Big Mac* right in front of this picture and leave the apartment for awhile. I bet when I come back — There will be nothing left but the wrapper!

Thanks for the reading Lisa. As I broke my gaze and looked back at my computer — these words were typed out on the screen.

I know him not — But yet I do
This man of vision and deep thought too

I know him not — But yet can see
A deep concern he tries to free

I know him not — But I can tell
His light shines bright and his shadows fell

I know him not — But he shall know
The Tarot cards are in his soul

I know him not — But once in time
My love was his and his was mine

~ Mona Lisa

Printed in Great Britain
by Amazon